Jarrad Reddekop

The Mournful Cage

Jarrad Reddekop

The Mournful Cage

Max Weber as a Hunger Artist

VDM Verlag Dr. Müller

Imprint

Bibliographic information by the German National Library: The German National Library lists this publication at the German National Bibliography; detailed bibliographic information is available on the Internet at http://dnb.d-nb.de.

Any brand names and product names mentioned in this book are subject to trademark, brand or patent protection and are trademarks or registered trademarks of their respective holders. The use of brand names, product names, common names, trade names, product descriptions etc. even without a particular marking in this works is in no way to be construed to mean that such names may be regarded as unrestricted in respect of trademark and brand protection legislation and could thus be used by anyone.

Cover image: www.purestockx.com

Publisher:
VDM Verlag Dr. Müller Aktiengesellschaft & Co. KG, Dudweiler Landstr. 125 a, 66123 Saarbrücken, Germany,
Phone +49 681 9100-698, Fax +49 681 9100-988,
Email: info@vdm-verlag.de

Copyright © 2008 VDM Verlag Dr. Müller Aktiengesellschaft & Co. KG and licensors
All rights reserved. Saarbrücken 2008

Produced in USA and UK by:
Lightning Source Inc., La Vergne, Tennessee, USA
Lightning Source UK Ltd., Milton Keynes, UK
BookSurge LLC, 5341 Dorchester Road, Suite 16, North Charleston, SC 29418, USA

ISBN: 978-3-8364-8506-7

Contents

1. Introduction		1
	Max Weber as a Hunger Artist	1
	The Suitors	3
2. Chapter I		13
	Weberian Addenda	16
	Responsible Technique	22
	Call and Vocation	26
3. Chapter II		31
	Rational Rejection	34
	World and Affirmation	40
	Loss and Memory	47
4. Chapter III		51
	The Wheel of History	54
	Infinite Abundance	60
	The Melancholic Will	66
5. Conclusion		71
6. Bibliography		73

Introduction

> *"Well, clear this out now!" said the overseer, and they buried the hunger artist, straw and all. Into the cage they put a young panther. Even the most insensitive felt it refreshing to see this wild creature leaping around the cage that had so long been dreary. The panther was all right. The food he liked was brought him without hesitation by the attendants; he seemed not even to miss his freedom . . . and the joy of life streamed with such ardent passion from his throat that for the onlookers it was not easy to stand the shock of it. But they braced themselves, crowded around the cage, and did not want ever to move away.*
>
> -Franz Kafka, A Hunger Artist[1]

Max Weber as a Hunger Artist

Two figures from Kafka call us to thinking as we inquire into the work of Max Weber, as we attempt to let resonate the fullness of his word. Let us recall, on the one hand, the figure of the hunger artist who perishes amidst the straw of his iron cage, finding that he could not help himself, that he *had* to fast – he who could never find any food he liked from amongst the abundant feasts which were nonetheless within his means. In the hunger artist we encounter no grandiose moralism, no *rejection* of eating – he should have liked nothing better than to gorge himself like anyone else, had only the food available not seemed somehow *empty*. It is rather that he found such naturalism impossible, being already somehow precluded; his art brings loss to disclosure from out of a thinking which senses already and everywhere that disappearance, but whose gesture suggests somehow the faithfulness of a remembrance. This is why no one could understand the hunger artist: those who could sense no emptiness within the abundance they enjoyed could only imagine that his fasting was a virtuoso performance of self-denial, *that in truth he only wanted what they themselves knew to bring satiety*. This was the secret jab of the impresario, who could always subdue the artist by making of his fast something altogether and harmlessly *comprehensible*, readily *explicable*: to praise his high ambition, his asceticism, and thereby *nullifying* his art and what was gathered in its gesture. For the

---

[1] Franz Kafka, "A Hunger Artist," in <u>Franz Kafka: The Complete Stories</u> ed. by Nahum N. Glatzer (New York: Schocken Books, 1971), 277.

spectators remain above all oblivious to that gesture as long as it is merely brought within that knowledge which keeps them secure, as long as it is not seen precisely to *withdraw* from any attempt to think it from out of that security.

Now I think that Weber is a hunger artist like this; and that we similarly fail to glimpse adequately his art so long as we merely refer to him as yet another repetition of all our favourite catechisms – theorizing a responsible freedom in modernity, finding some way of redeeming reason from its devastations, working out a position which delineates in advance what may be hoped, and how one ought best to act. Such a comforting reading is by no means uncommon, as we shall attempt to show. But no less does it disavow precisely what is most unsettling and most thoughtful in his work, which can see in such a rationalizing project the *rejection* of the world, an evisceration, an emptiness – and which simultaneously strives to leap away from that rejection. Paying heed more carefully to Weber's thought, we encounter the difficult challenge of letting resonate that hunger, that loss to which he gestures, that call to thinking which comes as *disenchantment*. It is this challenge which reveals most fully the *weightiness* of Weber's meditations upon technological culture and its expiations, which takes shape at once through a persistent brooding upon what belongs to rationalization *as* a kind of enclosed soteriology, ringed always by the darkness of an abyss, *and* in an attempt to listen most earnestly to the echoes of gods in their flight, to preserve in some sense the memory of their presence. To follow Weber down the path of his thinking forces our gaze unwaveringly upon a fundamental disjuncture disclosed at the core of rationalized existence; having been brought to inhabit that irrevocable tension, we come to know it as gallingly familiar, already present wherever the light of reason turns. For that too is what remains haunting within the artist's gesture: Weber exposes us to the viral force of that thinking which is technical, which cannibalizes as it renders clear, and which we find already manifest at each refined attempt to think our way out of its grip, even should we flee into silence. The challenge of Weber's thought lies in the ease with which, at every turn, he will smile and point to the frame of bars of the iron cage we had hoped to leave behind.

Kafka's text also proffers a second figure: for the dreary melancholy of the hunger artist, who had long since been not only misunderstood but altogether *forgotten*, is replaced by the very emblem of his disavowal, by the spectacular and oblivious vivacity of a caged panther. Where the hunger artist had disclosed an emptiness, a loss of "naturalism", the panther implicitly retains that loss as a figure of *rediscovery*: of the ferocity of the wild, of an abundance of appetite, a noble aspect, of "freedom", of ardent liveliness. But it is precisely that prior loss, that dreariness, which slides now into the oblivion of forgetfulness for the onlookers, whose morbid atrophy fades before a thrilling show of exuberance. The cage vanishes.

The panther is revealed in its character only in relation to the hunger artist whose burial it confirms. For it is precisely the pronounced lack of the artist's fast which brings us to see the great cat for what it is, which shows the morbidity implicit in its wildness, which reminds us of the cage we might nonetheless love to forget. In a similar way, Weber's story of loss shows up precisely the *rediscovered liveliness* inherent in our own celebrated attempts to enjoy the abundance we continually work to make available, to bring back whatever has been lost, to theorize freedom or fulfillment or even resistance within the permissive and stale orgy of late capitalism. Everywhere the ready feast turns to ash; Weber brings rather a vision of oblivion, of nihilism, and of disavowal, for which he also offers no palliative. Indeed, that vision unfolds as what comes to one who is called today to a thinking not simply "rational", which does not merely chant the refrains of liberalism, which questions seriously and with awe after the character of existence and yet which sees that very questioning cast out by the terms of our reasoned life. But that is also what marks Weber as a daring and serious thinker, and what brings him to resonate where one feels a gnawing *impoverishment* in the modern life which excites so many, where one *cannot* simply be drawn in by the enticements of the panther. For his thought also bears the character of faithfulness, drawing the hard consequences of reason's expiations and thus preserving in some way the integrity and profundity of his vision which takes on what perhaps is hardest – which glimpses the trail of gods, despite the agony that vision must bring today.

The Suitors

One nonetheless recurrently encounters, in the mountainous literature concerned with Weber's work, his recuperation as an ethicist of responsibility, theorizing the conditions and stakes of a mature and reasoned freedom in modernity. It may well be a mark of the discomforting nature of his thought that scholars should pursue again and again such a project; for in this way his challenge is quelled, in his comforting retrieval as one who runs the circuit from finitude to liberalism and so can confirm for us the appropriateness of such a position, and indeed the project of working-out which grants it, under the circumstances of modern life.

David Owen's book *Maturity and Modernity: Nietzsche, Weber, Foucault and the Ambivalence of Reason*, though a little over a decade old, offers an exemplary and fairly rigorous version of this general line of interpretation.[2] Weber's thinking, so the argument goes, must be understood to be grounded in a celebration of the autonomous individual as it has been constituted in and through the development of Puritan worldly asceticism and processes of rationalization. Such processes are shown to be fundamentally ambivalent, however, insofar as they simultaneously unleash the routinizing and specializing forces of bureaucratization, more "austerely rational" than any known in the past, which correspond to a refinement and generalization of instrumental calculation within the contemporary world. Such forces threaten to constitute a "shell of bondage" for the autonomous individual, making of him only a dull cog within a self-perpetuating machine of calculation. The central and motivating question of Weber's thought, then, is taken to be a kind of reasoning-out of the following concern, as it is voiced in *Economy and Society* and frequently quoted in readings of this kind:

> Given the basic fact of the irresistible advance of bureaucratization, the question about the future forms of political organization can only be asked in the following way . . . How can one possibly save *any remnants* of "individualist" freedom in any sense?[3]

For Owen, such a concern is given a correlative grounding in the epistemological and ontological predicates of Weber's methodological writings. Weber is thus cast as proceeding from a fundamental metaphysical position – and thus grounding knowledge in a particular conception of man as valuating subject, coming in the end to a familiar, if ultimately tautological, ethics of autonomy.[4]

Proceeding from such an orientation, Owen reads Weber as concerned to formulate an ethic of responsibility which would function as a form of resistance to (but not abolition of) the machinic forces of bureaucratization.[5] Owen posits a

---

[2] David Owen, Maturity and Modernity: Nietzsche, Weber, Foucault and the Ambivalence of Reason (New York: Routledge, 1994), esp. 84-139.
[3] Max Weber, Economy and Society: An Outline of Interpretive Sociology, Vol. 3, ed. by Guenther Roth and Claus Wittich, trans. by Ephraim Fischoff et al (New York: Bedminster Press Inc., 1968), 1403. Referenced in Owen's work on pg. 125.
[4] see Owen, Maturity and Modernity, 99.
[5] See esp. Owen, Maturity and Modernity, 125-133.

fundamental connection between the unified "personality" (which Weber connected to the worldly asceticism of the self-scrutinizing Puritan), and the occurrence as such of *charisma*, something of a counterforce to dry bureaucratization. In this way, the production of vocational man (specifically in the spheres of politics and science), charismatically possessed by the calling of his work and constituted as an autonomous self-reflexive subject, enables a resistance to instrumentality in the moment of the responsible decision of values.[6]

As we have suggested, such a reading is by no means uncommon.[7] And yet, one must concede that Weberian scholarship is at once vast and contested – one encounters all manner of divergent inflections. Perhaps we make our task too easy for ourselves insofar as we appear poised only to dispute the substance of one set of "interpretations" of *what Weber said*. For all manner of "alternatives" exist – other readings which plumb with varying emphases the works of Weber with an eye to *depicting accurately his description of the "fate of the times" and his response to it*. For instance: Kari Palonen finds cause to describe Weber's sense of "freedom" – which he is taken to in some way *celebrate* – as specifically *modern*, a "freedom of contingency", a room for play in which one has always the chance to act otherwise.[8]

---

[6] See Owen, Maturity and Modernity, 130-131. In the case of Owen's analysis, the further point is made that Weber's scientist and his politician form two contributing forces in the entrenchment/production of the autonomous individual in modern society – the politician creating "external" and the scientist "internal" conditions of possibility for such freedom. Weber's thinking is thus construed as working out, by way of a normative theorization of vocational man, a kind of quasi-solution to the predicament of his (and indeed, *our*) era.

[7] Some further examples include Duncan Kelly, who has more recently advanced a similar argument (indeed, drawing often upon Owen), seeing in Weber's description of vocational man a certain hope for a transvaluation of values in the face of instrumental meaninglessness, composed in such a way that it might, grasped as an ethics made exemplary by the politician and scientist, approach and be susceptible to generalization and institutionalization. Claus Offe's recent reading, is developed around the same quote from *Economy and Society* cited above, with the added inflection that Weber, in a quasi Tocquevillian appreciation of voluntary associations, might be read as celebrating turn-of-the-century America specifically as a locus of freedom. Alkis Kontos has also presented a variant of this analysis, notable here for its reformulation in terms of value-positing as "re-enchantment", in this way offering a dialectically teleological and quasi-comedic account of Weber's thinking on the iron cage of rationalized modernity. And a set of moves similar to Owen's may be found within Michael C. Williams' The Realist Tradition and the Limits of International Relations, which recovers the Weberian question of responsibility in the formulation of an ethic of "willful Realism" purged of melancholy. See Duncan Kelly, The State of the Political: Conceptions of Politics and the State in the Thought of Max Weber, Carl Schmitt and Franz Neumann (Oxford University Press, 2003), 22-73; esp. 53-8, 67; Claus Offe, "Max Weber: American Escape Routes From the Iron Cage?" in Reflections on America trans. by Patrick Camiller (Cambridge: Polity, 2005); Alkis Kontos, "The World Disenchanted, and the Return of Gods and Demons," in The Barbarism of Reason: Max Weber and the Twilight of Enlightenment ed. by Asher Horowitz and Terry Maley (University of Toronto Press: 1994), 223-248; Michael C. Williams, The Realist Tradition and the Limits of International Relations (Cambridge University Press: 2005).

[8] Kari Palonen, "Max Weber's Reconceptualization of Freedom," in Political Theory 27:4 (Aug. 1999).

For Lawrence A. Schaff, Weber teaches in his understanding of modernity the zealotry of "instrumental reason", to be resisted through a turn to aesthetic experience and the artistic avant-garde's search for the new.[9] For Harvey Goldman, Weber seeks to bring back a certain Puritan understanding of calling (as against the more mundane professionalism of his contemporary Germans) as a source of meaning where other anchors have faded. This formulation does not adopt the *language* of willful freedom but nonetheless preserves its central metaphysical problematic insofar as it is precisely the "world-mastering, innovating power", unique in origin to the West, which is to be celebrated and defended.[10] Wilhelm Hennis, by contrast, recounts Weber's "central problematic" as understanding the development of a special kind of humanity in modernity, in grasping the character of its "spirit". Once again, however, Weber's "response" is sought, in precisely such a way that having *articulated what we now are (i.e., the ground of our own action), Weber is to tell us what may be hoped* in a way which follows logically from the terms of that "whatness". We come thereby to celebrate modern politics as institutionally enabling the provocation of that kind of willful struggle which marks the excelling of human beings.[11] Or again, Wolfgang Mommsen has famously countered a series of "positivist" readings of Weber in order to find in him a series of lessons for political ethics under modern conditions, for a somehow better and normative understanding of how science and politics should be conceived to relate to one another.[12]

One might well go on in this direction. A thorough disputation of the findings of these or other scholars, however, belongs neither within the scope of this monograph nor within the interests of its author. And indeed, all of these interpreters seem to repeat with only minor divergences the central movements we have sought to draw to attention via the work of David Owen. Namely: i) each takes Weber, in "his response" to the fate of the times, as proceeding from a fundamentally metaphysical thinking of man (which becomes no less abstract in being merely *modern man*) in order to work out how he might come in some sense to flourish, which is at the same

---

[9] Lawrence A. Schaff, Fleeing the Iron Cage: Culture, Politics, and Modernity in the Thought of Max Weber (Berkeley: University of California Press, 1989).
[10] Harvey Goldman, Max Weber and Thomas Mann: Calling and the Shaping of the Self (Berkeley: University of California Press, 1988), esp. 168.
[11] Wilhelm Hennis, Max Weber, Essays in Reconstruction trans. by Keith Tribe (London: Allen & Unwin, 1988).
[12] Wolfgang J. Mommsen, Max Weber and German Politics 1890-1920 trans. by Michael S. Steinberg (Chicago: University of Chicago Press, 1959).

time to overcome the impediments represented by the constrictions of modernity. Indeed, these "constrictions" gain their character precisely *as* impediments to man's flourishing; ii) each, thus, takes up Weber in such a way as to find within his work redemptive lessons concerning some version of quasi-emancipatory "freedom"; iii) each works to acknowledge an eviscerating or annihilating force attendant to reason while simultaneously saving its central project, insisting upon the possibility of thinking our way out of the devastations of "modernity", of "technology", of "progress". What is crucial is that one always regains the possibility of thinking technique technically – as something to be used responsibly, brought under control, or even opposed, while all manner of foils may be invoked so as to preserve as intact the project of willful reordering *as such*. And indeed: in contrast to such movements one encounters in Weber something unique and subsequently rare – that is, an ability to draw us to the hard consequences of what was revealed to him in the emptiness of rationalized life, pushing forward the question of disenchantment to a point where one becomes precisely and inexorably *estranged* from technical thinking.

These "technical" encounters with Weber, we suggest, fail to take seriously the fullness of his thought, which rather dares us to let that evisceration assume all its weight, and not so readily spirit it away before the image of a "mature modernity". Moreover, one must ask how the very *mode* in which all of these authors interrogate Weber already does much of their work, already prepares us for their readings. All of those scholarly interpretations we have mentioned presume from the outset a project of *accurately portraying what Weber said, in such a way that one looks to find articulated within his thought a central ethical "position", a response, in some sense a "way out" of our problems* – which almost inevitably involves the invocation of some version of liberal freedom. Such analyses presume in their vision of Weber, and perform in their own analyses, certain understandings of man, of thought, and of how man is within the world. Such understandings, not unfamiliar to us within modernity, *proceed from the beginning from questions of knowledge.* Our scholars seek Weber's *point of view* – his knowledge and his reasoned ethics which belong to him *as a subject* (articulated predominantly along Kantian lines), and which speaks to the lives of others *who are also and only subjects*. But moreover, what is posited from the beginning is that *identity belongs to being* – i.e., that what we can determine *about* man, as a willful subject who knows, *is man* in such a way that it constitutes absolutely the beginning of what may be said and the scope of its trajectory. Taken together as a collection of truth-claims and assertions of value within identified problematics, Weber's thoughts can come to serve for us as things from which we might take instruction, or which we might debate or defend – in all events as something we may then "have" in some sense at our disposal in our own reasoning.

The movement of analysis, by virtue of this project, becomes almost identical in all the instances we have mentioned: one begins from what one may take to be Weber's definition, as it were, of modern man, and his correlative prescriptions for the present day and then projects them across the rest of his work – thus various facets of his sociological studies of religion in particular come (where they are mentioned at all) to gain highly peculiar inflections in order to be seen as *supporting evidence for his prescriptions, for the ethics he works out*. Moreover, one becomes familiar with the insinuation that what is *thought* in Weber's work is also identical with "what" he *said*, in the sense of being reducible to the metaphysical language used or with some self-conscious series of assertions concerning Weber's ultimate "project". All is done happily within the terms of reason; none entertain in the slightest the possibility that Weber might evince an attempt to *think out beyond such terms*. If limits exist at all to our grasp of Weber's thought it is as within a problem of quantifiable finitude – we simply don't have access to all of what he said. And indeed: insofar as one's scholarly intentions lie in disputing the accuracy of one version of Weber's position as against another, it may well prove a sensible method to mine the entirety of his notes for hidden proofs, to mourn what scribblings remain unpublished, to search for answers in all those documents in which he was meant to have spoken, frankly, the truth of his project.[13]

To repeat: what seems presumed in such a mode of questioning is the insistence that one may apply the metaphysical preconditions for such a "position" back upon the thinker himself – i.e., we suppose that Weber's thought must conform to the dictates of the knowledge we would seek to have about it. What else can such scholarly contestations over *accuracy* with regards to Weber presume but that one may simply recognize in the form of an ultimate and clarified *point of view* the truth of his thought and that this truth should be non-contradictory? Indeed, would we not

---

[13] As an extreme example, we might cite Wilhelm Hennis, who (in a methodologically peculiar manoeuvre) opted to investigate Weber's applications for grant money as a privileged site for learning just what Weber was *really* doing, as a source for proclamations which may be taken at face value. See Hennis, 52-5.

suppose, in seeking Weber's own confessions concerning his project precisely a strange understanding of the thinker as self-identical with the reasoned thought he is meant to present – in short, do we not make of him a quasi-Puritan ascetic and presume that he suffers thereby *no loss whatsoever?*

To take Weber seriously as a hunger artist, it seems, one must pursue altogether a different mode of questioning. For it is precisely the Weber who *unsettles* such rationalized thinking that interests us, whose thought inhabits most profoundly an experience of tension. By "tension", moreover, we mean not simply an aporia or irreconcilibility as between two *ethical positions,* but precisely an experience of *melancholia* attendant to this kind of reasoning-out of positions as such. Thus we seek to glimpse precisely those aspects of his thought for which his own metaphysical language (whether as scientist or as political theorist) was glaringly insufficient – and in relation to which that insufficiency became markedly *present.* In this way – by letting resonate the sense of loss to which Weber gestures in his work – we allow his thought to come more fully to disclosure.

We do not approach our study, however, in such a way that our case would be proved upon finding a sentence in Weber's diary declaring, "I have always intended my work to be a kind of hunger artistry." If the image of the "hunger artist" may be misleading, it is in exaggerating a sense of *intention*, referring to what Weber *self-consciously and deliberately did as the producer of his work.* Such a language of willfulness, however, seems not particularly helpful for articulating what it is that we "do" as thinkers, or the way in which we question after things which lay claim to us and draw us along. Moreover, to prove in some way the degree to which Weber "knew" what he was doing would seem to demand that one pose a number of questions and presume much which would tend only to obscure, if not to block altogether, the course of our inquiry. Our attempt to take Weber *as* a hunger artist here, instead, aims to draw attention to the way in which his work nonetheless *evinces* a particular movement of questioning. Through following that movement, one comes more fully to understand even those moments of tension and passion in which Weber remained quite caught up, and in which he did indeed propose an ethics of responsibility. We seek, however, to hearken to what is gathered, and not merely asserted, in Weber's saying. Kafka's hunger artist aids us in drawing into emphasis that gathering and to contemplate its character.

But we must note that our aim in questioning is not merely to better represent "Weber", to increase our historical knowledge of him. Why, in seeking to understand the hunger artist, should we merely treat him as an object of knowledge, simply ignoring at all costs the very challenge of his thinking, and placing him harmlessly amongst our compendia of the dissected? Why should our own habitual sense of what is done in a scholarly vocation be permitted to remain undisturbed in this encounter? Does not an attempt to hear and take seriously the call Weber would think through "disenchantment" demand rather something quite different?

In *Identity and Difference,* Heidegger writes: "When thinking attempts to pursue something that has claimed its attention, it may happen that on the way it undergoes a change. It is advisable, therefore, in what follows to pay attention to the path of thought rather than its content."[14] Dwelling only upon "content", which *as content* must belong to a thinking from out of metaphysically-given terms, one would seem already and continually to back away from "what" is thought, to establish before it a distance. In thinking the call of disenchantment in what follows, therefore, it would seem to defeat in advance our efforts to speak only of Weber's *claims*, and the claims we would seek to make about them, to reduce the echoes of gods to one such claim (and thus already deafen ourselves to them). Rather, we attempt ourselves to follow the path of Weber's thought; we ourselves must learn what it is to listen to the beckoning of gods in their withdrawal. In so doing, we seek to follow him towards a more fundamental questioning after the character of our being – and thus towards an articulation of our era which extends much further than what may attend a comparative discussion of "points of view".

This does not mean that we merely abandon all rigour in thinking: rather we seek to follow only more closely Weber's thought. But neither need we disavow the sense in which this study is undertaken less for the sake of a knowledge about Weber than *because something like disenchantment also claims our own thinking.* Considering ourselves in light of his thought, I suggest, we encounter something which seems to manifest and crystallize a set of fundamental dilemmas in which we continue to reside – and which are so poorly articulated in the terms of our accustomed language. We are concerned not merely with the man, therefore, but with his word, and this because we find ourselves strikingly at home within it. Thus that

---

[14] Martin Heidegger, Identity and Difference trans. by Joan Stambaugh (University of Chicago Press, 2002), 23.

we aim to show that, in the movements of Weber's thought, one glimpses in all its profundity the contours of a horizon we continue to inhabit – i.e., that *he names in a fundamental way our own era – fundamental because it bears upon the way being and beings lend themselves to thought as such.* In this way, we aim to let resonate in all its force the gesture of Weber's hunger artistry – to do justice to what comes to thought in his *melancholy*[15], and moreover to that very call of disenchantment which also draws us along.

A final suggestion might be added here, which builds upon what has been said. Owen's account, as I have tried to show, is significant because he manages to subdue Weber's disquiet through a series of manoeuvres one encounters much more broadly. The space is not available here to elaborate and adequately defend the claim; but I would nevertheless suggest that one sees time and again in subsequent thought an *approach* towards Weber's "problem", often as a gnawing sense of the violences of reason, but always in the end an aversion, an escape from the final implications, from the profound *tension* Weber could inhabit. Not infrequently does this escape manifest as the saving of "politics" and the (metaphysical) possibility of its theorization: one reverts to a language of power and resistances, or of an emancipatory ethic where the forces of bondage mark a disruption of the equilibria of reason, or an impediment of what belongs properly to man as productive. Thus Foucault, for whom Heidegger could be "the essential philosopher", could still locate the vocation of the intellectual in apprehending properly what belongs to "today" so as to perceive "space[s] of concrete freedom, that is, of possible transformation," – we encounter the familiar

---

[15] It should be noted that the terms *melancholy* and *mournfulness* in this monograph are not used in reference to Freudian and subsequent psychoanalytic definitions of (and distinctions between) the terms. A weighing-in on such conversations belongs neither within the scope our book or its aim; and particularly distracting in our context would be an attempt to think our words in terms of the pathologies or functions of the subject, as a mapping of *desire*, transferences of emotions, etc. Thus by *mournfulness* and *melancholy* we do *not* mean either a grieving for a lost *object*, or a more vague sense of loss internalized within the ego. If the Freudian discussion is at all helpful, it may be insofar as one might cast both our terms as in some sense inhabiting a space somewhere between (if we may thus simplify the discussion) the poles of i) a less distinct sense of loss and ii) the loss of an object. For in a sense (as we will show) Weber's loss both takes the flight of the gods *seriously* (though not, anachronistically, as *real*) and yet precisely does not take them as *objects* which might be reclaimed or substituted for. Much closer, however, to our sense of *melancholy* and *mournfulness* is Walter Benjamin's in <u>The Origin of the German Tragic Drama</u> trans. by John Osbourne. (New York: Verso, 1998) – though this text makes ventures towards questions of redemption which we aim to avoid. But here, both terms belong, in much the same sense, to the way in which modern man "betrays the world for the sake of knowledge", and invoke an interplay of betrayal/loss with a mode of faithfulness, in mourning, "to the world of things". (157)

vision of the empiricist whose groundwork prepares for the production of change.[16] Deleuze similarly takes up Heidegger's "problem" of identity/difference while precisely *preserving philosophy*, working out a kind of messianic ethics of care in relation to that "sense" which *inheres within propositions* – thus one may unify potentiality and actuality without being estranged from that "enframing" whereby one thinks the world in some way in relation to the securing of propositional truth itself, and thus from out of questions of *knowledge*.[17] In Giorgio Agamben, we likewise see an attempt to take up the question of technique only to retain at bottom a messianic language, finally manifest in a "coming struggle" of humanity against the "alienation of language as such", particularly as it is manifest in the *state*.[18]

As much as Weber's "problem" would seem to haunt us, no less does the final disjuncture of his thinking remain eschewed, which avoidance so often resides in a reversion to our old sense of vocation and reasoned hope. In such a context, however, we would seem to do well to take seriously Weber's challenge, as the discomforting figure who reveals always the panther and the cage, but in so doing comes to name something all the more compelling, all the greater in insight, at once intimately near to us and terrifying. It is to let resonate *this* Weber, to follow him down the darkest and most luminous paths of his thought, which we attempt here.

In Chapter I, we shall attempt to throw the image of the panther back upon contemporary technological culture and its attendant search after the possibility of "responsibility". Chapter II will ask after what is disavowed by such pantherine thought – that is, we shall follow the convolutions and paradoxes of Weber's thought on disenchantment. In Chapter III, we will return to Weber's vocational lectures and his methodological thought in order to bring out the *tensions* and the *remembrances* which lie within his thought on "responsibility", and thus to pay heed to his *melancholy*, to the bitter insight and expansive vision of Weber's word.

---

[16] See Michel Foucault, "Structuralism and Post-structuralism," in Foucault: Aesthetics, Method, and Epistemology ed. by James Faubion trans. by Robert Hurley et al (New York: The New Press, 1998), esp. 449-50. On this point we may also compare Jean Baudrillard's helpful discussion in Forget Foucault (New York: Semotext(e), 1987), esp. 34-44.
[17] I am thinking particularly here of The Logic of Sense, ed. by Constantin V. Boundas and Mark Lester (Columbia University Press, 1990).
[18] See especially Giorgio Agamben, Means Without End: Notes on Politics trans. by Vincenzo Binetti and Cesare Casarino (University of Minnesota Press, 2000). The above quote is from 96.

Chapter I

Not summer's bloom lies ahead of us, but rather a polar night of icy darkness and hardness, no matter which group may triumph externally now... When this night shall have slowly receded, who of those for whom spring apparently has bloomed so luxuriously will be alive? And what will have become of all of you by then? Will you be bitter or banausic? Will you simply and dully accept world and occupation? Or will the third and least frequent possibility be your lot: mystic flight from reality for those who are gifted for it, or – as is both frequent and unpleasant – for those who belabour themselves to follow this fashion?

-Max Weber, *Politics as a Vocation*[19]

Max Weber's grim vision of an iron cage of rationalized existence, a long winter of bleak stillness despite the semblance of "external" change, developed as part of a prolonged meditation upon the experience of "senselessness" within contemporary life. Such was the condition, he argued, of life emancipated by reason from the various forms of traditionalism and "naïveté", by the construction and differentiation of values *qua* values and the refinement of technical means for their pursuit. Senselessness could loom as the latent abyss within a culture predicated upon the articulation of the meaning of the world, of action, of selves, and the subsequent systematization – that is, rationalization – of thought, of conduct, of life itself. Such processes are of course much older than those collection of centuries we are accustomed to calling modern; Weber found roots of specifically "Western" forms of rationality in Zoroastrian, Jewish, Roman, and Christian religion, amongst others. But the articulation and hence the separation of value-spheres – thus the rupture of any organic, "full" sense of living – is accomplished, for Weber, to the greatest extent in modern culture. The Weberian story broods upon the *loss* suffered by modern man, upon the terrible desolation of his expiatory and intellectualizing liberation. For it is in modernity that we encounter in its highest development the emptiness of the

---

[19] Max Weber, "Politics as a Vocation," in From Max Weber: Essays in Sociology Trans. and ed. by H.H. Gerth and C. Wright Mills (Routledge: 1957), 128.

constructive will to management and the accompanying systematization of the self into which we are forced by life under capitalism.[20]

Perhaps more specifically, Weber's analysis shows up a relationship between the loss of naïveté, senselessness, and the thinking of existence from out of principles of *knowledge* made clear before the intellect. His formal expression of disenchantment offered in *Science as a Vocation* – as the showing up of all things as calculable *in principle* – points to the way in which the thingness of things can show up in their intelligibility where the conditions of that intelligibility are clear and grant it shape from out of a prior lawfulness. Weber had earlier (in *Economy and Society*) described as disenchanting any thinking which reduced existence to questions of meaning[21]; but his later formulation reflects a pronounced contextualization within late modernity, where we can see that thought comes to be justified before itself in relation to particular problematics of obtaining certainty from out of doubt. It is here that the *essentia* of man stands to be determined in the constitution of the subject as willful, as *productive* and clear in that productivity before himself, over and against which objects can stand in their realness as calculable processes of efficient causality to be marshaled in their effects in accordance with posited ends. With disenchantment, Weber names that very thinking within which the "problematics" of science and politics come to take shape within modernity and recall one another, and show in themselves a cultivated apprehension of what is from out of a prepared ground of reasoned knowledge.

The development of modern understandings of relations between fact and value, and its relationship to soteriological imperatives, follows a long and convoluted course in Weber's work which we shall attempt to trace more fully in Chapter Two. But it is in drawing this fundamental connection – between contemporary questions of (competing) values, the development and pre-eminence of science as a mode of encountering the real, processes of rationalization and a latent salvation ethic predicated upon the *rejection* of being, that Weber forces us to draw the hard consequences for that thinking which would seek to re-order the world. That project of constructive rationality which renders calculable, whose generalization would seem

---

[20] An excellent exposition by Weber on these issues is to be found towards the end of his essay "Religious Rejections of the World and Their Directions," in From Max Weber: Essays in Sociology, esp. 355-8.
[21] E.g., Max Weber, Economy and Society: An Outline of Interpretive Sociology, trans. by Ephraim Fischoff et al., ed. by Guenther Roth and Claus Wittich (New York: Bedminster Press, 1968), 506.

to mark for us irresistibly the task of thought in late modernity, is thus offered a glimpse of its implacable and attendant loss. This is a loss, in the end, not simply of "sense" but of what must be rejected for the world to be reduced to the stamp of meaning at all.

Recalling Kafka's story of the hunger artist, it may be that we today, like the spectators before the fasting man, have little time for such a melancholic display. Perhaps we prefer the pantherine imagery of health, of life rediscovered – of oblivious vivacity, easily fed, "leaping around the cage that had so long been dreary." Indeed: when so many perish of *actual starvation*, who has time for one who simply couldn't find the food he liked?[22] But we must be careful here too lest we have eyes only for the panther – for we know that "liking" too stands to be seized upon, and would fly in a moment in search of measure and causal analyses, that we might better make that liking available. To take stock of the portent of Kafka's figures, we must ask after their significance as a vision of rationalized culture, and their relation to the very ways in which processes of rationalization reinstall themselves. The sheer abundance of scholarship today on the devastations of technological "progress" would seem to evince not only an acute awareness of the eviscerations of reason, but also an insistence upon *thinking our way out of them* – of divorcing reason from its wasteland and making possible a clean re-invention of progress, a refined management. Kafka's panther, I suggest, belongs to the ways we come to see technique as something technical, as an injunction to further research, as something to be controlled and used *responsibly*.

In this chapter, then, we shall attempt to throw the image of the panther back upon the imperatives of research, to show up the ways the will to management reinvigorates itself at every turn. Weber's thought, as we will come to show, inhabits a dissonance whose condition is the way the *experience* of disenchantment makes torturous in a certain way both action in the rationalized world as much as inaction. Before we question after the nature of Weber's melancholy, however, we must attend to the means of its *disavowal*, to the hiding of the iron cage which nonetheless endures all the more resolutely. In this vein, we will come to focus upon the question of responsibility – such a question is central not only for showing how Weber's recuperation as a reconciled ethicist belongs to his (comfortable) *rediscovery*, but for

---

[22] Kafka, "A Hunger Artist," 277.

delineating how *responsibility as ethics as such* belongs to that very disavowal by means of which his most profound thinking is committed to oblivion.

Weberian Addenda

How must we append the Weberian story, if this is indeed the long hour of its disavowal? Weber's *The Protestant Ethic and the Spirit of Capitalism* describes the role of Puritan and Calvinist predestinarian theology in the development of the vocational asceticism required by capitalism. This asceticism, in which the sober intellect strove against "the spontaneous enjoyment of life and all it had to offer," aimed towards the ordering of a subject capable of giving a unified and systematic account of itself, regulated by the ideal that all action might proceed from motives made clear before the intellect and oriented towards the rational labour of a "calling". [23] Implicit in the Puritan formulation was a rigorous war of self-conscious intention against the emotions, a reduction of the messiness of one's being to the clarity of the thought-image. This inner-worldly asceticism, for Weber, drew upon the psychological consequences of seeking the impossible certainty of a supramundane grace, predicated upon the rejection of the world, of leisure, of the "full and beautiful humanity" which could better co-exist even with Catholic cycles of sin and confession.[24] Today, however, leisure has been rediscovered on the market as the hallmark of healthy bourgeois living; the ascetic subject, once unified, finds itself capable of administering to all varieties of needs – spiritual, recreational, sexual, ecological, et cetera ad nauseam. Protestant asceticism has been humanized for the utilitarian consumer-subject; today a vocation may be hybridized or diversified – so much the better for the unified subject who may acknowledge his own complexity. Today we labour less to destroy an old abundance than to enjoy a rainbow of opportunities, to enter into the mundane, ironic salvation of the free leisure class, newly-sprouted from the ground of an old *ressentiment*.

The Protestant Ethic concludes by gesturing to the fading of "religious and ethical meaning" in capitalist life, to the retreat of the "spirit of religious asceticism" from the cage it had helped to build. As Heidegger would later see in America the "concentrated rebound" of the spirit of European nihilism, so for Weber the United

---

[23] Max Weber, The Protestant Ethic and the Spirit of Capitalism trans. by Talcott Parsons (New York: Charles Scribner's Sons, 1958), esp. 166, 117-124.
[24] Ibid, 117, 181.

States could embody the highest development of rationalizing capitalism, where the pursuit of wealth, devoid of any larger sense of meaning, "tends to become associated with purely mundane passions, which often actually give it the character of sport."[25] We would do well to ask, however, whether there is not some fundamental connection between the ongoing refinements of a rationalized management ethic, which extend far beyond mere matters of wealth, and the development of that sense of sport, to which the excitements of a rediscovered leisure would seem to belong.

Weber himself pointed to the way in which a developing rationalization had need to carve for itself new loci for the reinvention of what it had annulled: it is *after* the flight of the gods that one delineates a properly "religious" sphere for "religious experience"; it is *after* the loss of the confessional cycle that one must seek *proof* of God's grace through a worldly asceticism in the pursuit of wealth. That development, unfurling alongside a technological will to mastery for which all things could stand as fungible resource, could seem to tend inexorably *towards the mundane*. And indeed – it is perhaps hardly surprising that such an inexorable sentiment should continue to haunt a culture which masters the *real* in its empirical objectness as such. For so much seems only proper to a thinking taking shape from out of a theological heritage by which a world of dead matter, governed by laws of efficient causality, stood precisely *removed* from God its *creator*.[26]

Further, Weber could show how a movement of banalization could accompany the progression of science as a mode of encountering the real. In laying a framework by means of which one could give reasoned, rigorous accounts of truths about the world, science proved to be irreconcilable with older forms of "ethical religiosity": setting itself as the reasoned standard by which factual "accounts" of the world could be gauged, science could signal the further retreat of the old and other "value-systems", which suddenly come to show themselves *as* value-systems while simultaneously growing pale under the lens of factuality.[27] Because there is no

---

[25] Ibid, 181-2. The reference to Heidegger is from "What Are Poets For?" in Poetry, Language, Thought trans. by Albert Hofstadter (New York: Perennial, 2001), 111.

[26] A good account of this relationship between science as Christian theology stressing the *distance* of God from his *creation* – as over and against the "residual paganism" of an Aristotelian doctrine of essences, wherein the "only partial" separation of god and "nature" could justify the *a priori* methods of Aristotelian science – is given by M.B. Foster, "The Christian Doctrine of Creation and the Rise of Modern Natural Science," in Mind 43:172 (Oct. 1934), esp. 456-7.

[27] See Weber, "Religious Rejections of the World and Their Directions," 354-5. This movement also marks the significance of Plato's discovery of the "concept" in Weber's discussion in "Science as a Vocation," in From Max Weber, 141. A helpful discussion is also given by Bradley Bryan,

objective basis for value, any claim to value must rest upon the activity of the subject and its world-view; value is produced as value from out of a thinking which also gives "fact", which seeks to render clear the world in its reality on the basis of the presumption that it is rationally intelligible.[28]

What is significant about the notion that life in the world should attain the quality of sport, however, lies precisely in the way in which sport describes not simply the "real", but the way in which the real is already bound up with the play of willfulness, which enables the work of its imaginative reinvention. "World as sport" describes a mode of relating to things in which they bear the character of the small, the imaginatively produced, the way the *ordered* is at the same time the already *entertaining*. What is described is the point at which the question of value, called forth by a world of fact, comes already to bear in principle upon all things; it is the sign of the will to mastery coming to glimpse as supreme the principle of valuation itself. One encounters at one and the same time a world at once supremely calculable and absurdly fantastic, mastered and grotesquely (entertainingly) reworked. The very sleep that is reason itself produces monsters.

Sport bears the mark at once of rationalization, and an invented dynamics of play granted from out of a transparent lawfulness; but it connotes also a smallness, a boundedness: sport is only sport, it is perhaps war in miniature, it is play. But whereas sport may once have imitated war, it is now preserved as entertainment, a simulation enjoyed for itself; and no less does war, which is to be made safe through technological advancement, come to be attain a certain character as a form of entertainment. Not only cosmopolitans in search of peace are capable of asking: "what is the value of war?" Sport has been *decided* upon – it recycles the real and in so doing brings it altogether under the sign of value: sport, as having been invented, takes its shape only and insofar as it is desirable. "World *as* sport" points to a relation between a setting-forth upon the real and processes of *reinvention* whereby all things are brought already into relation with what is secured as productive – i.e., with the will which valuates. Resonant throughout, however, is an attendant *banalization* by which the world, abandoned by the gods, takes shape from out of the terms of a

---

"Postmodernism and the Rationalization of Liberal Legal Culture." Discussion paper D98-9, Eco-Research Chair of Environmental Law and Policy, University of Victoria (August 1998). Available at: <http://www.polisproject.org/polis2/Discussion%20Papers/D98-9-PoMoLiberalLegalCulture.pdf>
[28] Again, see the article by M.B. Foster above for a helpful discussion of the convolutions by which modern science could take shape as a particular form of rationalism implicit in the constitution of the *empirical* character of the object.

knowledge by which the real and the will are secured as such, just as what had once been the terrible plenitude of being's *fantasia* is now secured and made small as only the *fantasies* of the imagination which *represents*.[29]

Heidegger may have been correct in seeing in the emerging culture of the twentieth century a certain glib satisfaction at being no longer endangered; but a will grown weak will also make shows of strength. Liberalism may be a boring lover, enamoured always with the bounded language of domesticity and with the normal situation; but for that reason it is also imaginative. Baudrillard was right to take television and Disneyland so seriously as marking emergent modes of experience. Once again, "reality television" programs like *Survivor* are significant here not because they merge the everyday with a rediscovered excitement within the demarcated sphere of *fantasy*, or even because the distinction between reality and artifice is retained within them only enough to produce allure while being entirely reversible (the plot is simultaneously about real people in outlandish imagined scenarios, and about artifice-driven Westerners getting back in touch with their real nature – it doesn't matter which, but the drawing of the dichotomy here has as its orientation above all the stimulation of drives). Their significance lies rather in a ruse which suggests that this is not how we are already living, that it is only entertainment; whereas that very logic of entertainment itself already governs experience more broadly within a world permeated by tourism and capitalism, in which all things stand in principle as *resource*, in which reality and its others circulate in endless permutation above all as excitation to the principle of valuation itself. Whatever excites the humours: and why not? A managerial ethic predicated upon rendering all things available under the sign of *value* soon turns to strange recycling, and in so doing makes its pact with caricature, which after all is stimulating to the imagination. What is crucial here, however, is that we see how the *mundane* comes to assume a character of the *extravagant*, the *colourful*, the *permissive, the thrilling*. One loves a little agitation: a little poison makes for agreeable dreams. Sport gains the character of exuberant liveliness within and for the boundedness of the iron cage.

Everything stands as resource: and so one is able to dream that anything one may imagine may be possible, may be made available. An impulse towards the

---

[29] This transition from fantasia to fantasy is discussed memorably in Martin Heidegger, "The Age of World Picture," in The Question Concerning Technology and Other Essays trans. by William Lovitt (New York: Harper & Row, 1977), 147.

emancipatory play of the imagination set free on the world would seem to at once betray a deeper *ambivalence* towards it, as has been implicit within modern delineations of a properly autonomous "aesthetic" sphere and the constitution of the "imagination" as such.[30] One may well oscillate between expansive imagining (because already bounded) and calls for the reasoned control of an ethics; but no less does one continue to inhabit a tension fundamental to modernity itself, which evinces the marriage of the will to know with the will to *fantasy*, with the inventive whims and dreams of the *subject*.[31] In this way the grotesque and the most expertly reasoned dance together locked in a Möbius embrace, fetishistic capitalism and technology (which is rather supported than contravened by a concomitant fetishism of *fact* and the staunch groundwire of the expert).

Thus the same logic which pushes forward the march of science would seem to be haunted also by a fetishism of the miniature, the bounded, the entertaining, the exotic. But even the chaotic, the torturous, the abusive have their genre: thus war and its sublimation can merge and become indistinguishable as a monstrous entertainment; again: a little poison makes for stimulating reveries. One may well enjoy playing upon a line endlessly productive once the sides are drawn: how close to life can the funhouse get, or how close to game is life? But perhaps these visions are already only tantalizing because, as caricature, they foreground a fiction which speaks of a deeper groundedness: whereas that very question of groundedness belongs to the way in which we *have come already and unavoidably to inhabit reason's funhouse*. This very way of bracketing belongs precisely to sport *as* sport and belongs to the play of its preservation, though our existence should come all the more to evince within its nature the phantasmagoric churnings of morbid reinvention.

But Weber's pronouncement foregrounds precisely a paucity here, a lack marked by the retreat of God and the gods: whereas Protestantism and its active

---

[30] See, for instance, Anthony Cascardi's discussion of the form of the novel as arising in relation to and expressing modern modes of encountering an increasingly disenchanted world marked by the split of subject and object in The Subject of Modernity (Cambridge University Press, 1992), esp. 105-7.

[31] The convolutions and complexities of this interrelation are no doubt far too complex to treat adequately here. My aim in the present text is merely to gesture towards that relation as an essential feature of the technological logic itself, with which one must grapple if one is to seek to understand psycho-sociologically the nihilism of late capitalism. No doubt much more could be written, for instance, concerning the *messianic* possibilities of theorizing a *redemptive* accord between something like the law and the breath – i.e., between a sense of *abundance* thought in connection with a sense of something like the "aesthetic" (in post-Kantian terms) and the truth of a rational knowledge presumed as prior. In this way, it seems to me, one might propose to read such thinkers as Deleuze (virtualities), Benjamin (profane illumination), and Agamben (Pauline messianism) as working out versions of "ethics" which remain *internal* to the central aesthetic-assertional axes of technology itself.

asceticism in search of a *certitudo salutis* had marked a further development in a spirit of rationalizing world-rejection, a world as sport is a world rendered all the more mundane, as intellectualized as it is entertaining and somehow empty. And yet, one might also say that it belongs to the entire constellation, as it does to sport, that one happily bracket what is marked to the outside: the terms of our life are what they are; why be concerned? No doubt what is bracketed slides readily into irrelevance or an oblivion: for what a fabulous game this is, which may be constantly refined so as to encompass anything! Even God and the gods may be brought back in, as grounding *value*, as having *value*. Pantherine vivacity comes to bloom within the iron cage in a way which belongs to its very logic; this is shown up in Weber's own sense of the impoverishment and the inexorable spread of that intellectualization which thinks what is from out of the dictates of lawful knowledge.

One may well find *proof* within such a technological framework of the Christian metaphysics of willfulness which it presupposes and with which it is bound, offering the comfort of a tautology. Such comforts (which grant a reasoned justification for the activities demanded by a world shaped by reason) may certainly grant reconciliation – if not any reprieve – from injunctions of rendering decision, of rethinking, of inhabiting life as a subject in the world today.[32] Indeed, and as Weber himself comes to show, that science by which the world today is *explained* and a rationalized politics of decision recall one another both in principle and in their historical development, insofar as processes of rationalization come to write a metaphysics of willfulness into the world with the force of necessity, constituting precisely the terms of serious engagement today. Knowledge, clarified for itself as representation by a subject made secure before himself as one who *posits* from out of *doubt*, lands one in principle within the modern political problematics of decision, with which we have been familiar since Hobbes.

Questions of fact call forth questions of value: and indeed, Weber himself offers a familiar articulation *in principle* of the activity of the subject as prior: one implicitly decides *that* a particular form of knowledge is worth having.[33] In bringing questions of *decision*, of *choice* to bear upon all things, one is cast already into

---

[32] An excellent account of the relationship between a metaphysics of willfulness and modern understandings of the real *qua* material is given by M.B. Foster, "Christian Theology and Modern Science of Nature II," in Mind 45:177 (January 1936), 1-28.
[33] See "Science as a Vocation," esp. 144-5.

resentment and a fall into banality, as Nietzsche saw: one can learn who and what is to blame, and how to *correct* our existence; in grasping the world as calculable *in principle* one prepares already to make it agreeable. The real takes shape from out of the intelligible which becomes already the valuable; before it, even the profundity that had once been able to come to thought in connection with the old "anchors of meaning" slips quietly away.

Perhaps Weber spoke too soon when he wrote the following:

> After Nietzsche's devastating criticism of those 'last men' who 'invented happiness,' I may leave aside the naïve optimism in which science – that is, the technique of mastering life which rests upon science – has been celebrated as the way to happiness. Who believes in this? – aside from a few big children in university chairs or editorial offices. Let us resume our argument.[34]

For where a logic of management continually reinstalls itself, it may indeed be much harder to find individuals who would *not*, in the last analysis, mouth such a confession of belief today. If the world is not, indeed, consistently improving in measurable ways, and if the agreeable and those routes which make available its efficient production are not somehow palatable – how miserable one must be, on whom the weight of decision gallingly hangs!

Responsible Technique

But if Weber's dismissal of the last men seems too early, we can see that he also offers the very formula of management itself in that dismissal. Small wonder, perhaps, that it should be precisely this formula for which Weber has come to stand in so many reclamations: as a liberal, as one who can find for us the heroic moment of decision which is redeeming, a space of creativity amidst routine, where (as amongst the last men) we may feel so often that there is none. And indeed: in the context of Weber's vocational lectures, the last man stands to be overcome in his *naivety* in the same way that a dry world of the bureaucratic calculation of efficient means may be in some sense redeemed – through the creative and (in principle) political moment of the positing of ends, i.e., of value. That moment of decision is to take upon itself the

---

[34] Weber, "Science as a Vocation," 143.

weight of the *ambivalence* of reason, thus presumably banishing the oblivious happiness of the last man through *cognizance*.[35]

It is perhaps a strange moment that attempts to overcome both the last man and the eviscerations of instrumentality through a return to the essential condition of a rational managerial ethic: the active subject, clear before himself. A creativity is theorized and made secure within the subject as that which can produce redemption for a life of dry routine; proceeding from an assertion of what belongs properly to man as productive, as a whatness clear to (specifically modern forms of) knowledge, the (free) willful subject may come rightfully into his own. Weber himself saw that such a moment, insofar as it belonged to a kind of self-clarification, stood "in the service of 'moral' forces" – which, in the larger context of his work, shows itself thereby as a force of *evisceration*, in the tradition of Puritan ethics, and which belongs perfectly to the way we have seen the imagination stand in some sense as bounded and thus available to rational scrutiny in modernity.[36] Indeed, Weber's figures of the scientist and the politician (which remain here metaphysically the same) seem not so much to overcome the figure of the last man as flesh him out sociologically within the context of a rationalized world. Politics, as the realm for the invention of meaning in a meaningless world – a meaning-machine – may well, as a site of creativity and struggle, provide some sense of respite from the dullness of bureaucratic life, but it does so in a manner *in principle internal to the mechanisms of eviscerating rationalization as such*.

Indeed, it seems as though such a formulation of the selection of ends assumes today less the raiment of hope than the garb of peddlers and ideologists. The choice of values, after all, would seem to confront us in a proliferation of contexts so extensive as to verge on the utterly banal. Such is our lot in our era of permissive capitalism and biotechnological harvest, with its continuous expansion of possibilities for the manipulation of life, predicated upon the principle of disenchantment itself, that nothing stands outside of relation to the calculative understanding of the will – or, indeed, of subjection to the will's capacity to choose. Thus living things can be

---

[35] C.f., for instance, Weber, "Politics as a Vocation," 127; and Weber, "Science as a Vocation," esp. 152, 155. Note in this last precisely the way in which both the weight of a sense of disenchantment and the spectre of the last men seem in some way mitigated by the moment of "a decisive choice" of value on the part of the scientist, which bears connection to the way in which he is forced to make account of himself and his conduct, "bringing about self-clarification and a sense of responsibility."
[36] Weber, "Science as a Vocation," 152.

shown in their factuality as *encoded programs,* producing statistically measurable effects to be managed, improved, altered.[37] Everything can stand as an object of willed production: and is this not precisely the language of invented happiness itself?

The mere repetition of the formula concerning ends and means, therefore, would seem hardly edifying within such a context. One may, no doubt, with its aid come to be reconciled to what one is already at work doing (indeed, precisely *redeeming* it – and what after all may *not* thereby be reduced to questions of political agency?), or perhaps inspired to push forward that very logic that already governs (hence, I suggest, Terry Maley's celebration of Weber's *politicization* of knowledge as opening new vistas of *freedom*).[38] But it may also be that we have made the question too easy for ourselves; for Weber's moment of decision also attains to a kind of heroic grandeur, in a way which takes more onto itself than we would seem to have expressed. The moment of decision, on the one hand, is marked precisely by a mindfulness of the ambivalence of rationalization and instrumentality. Thus, especially in connection with the figure of the politician, one who takes up the moment of decision "lets himself in for the diabolic forces lurking in all violence"; he must pact with the devil in working to do good.[39] That moment is marked by a tension implicit within the ethical paradox of politics itself: that life in the world is irreconcilable with the ultimate ends of salvation, and good on earth does not come from good alone. The ambivalence of reason, in this context, is shown up in a tragic mindfulness of *violence*, for which one may strive to be *responsible*. The oblivious happiness of the last men would seem tempered by a better understanding of what attends to *invention* as such, by an ethic of consequence.

We wish to suggest, however, that the opposition between ultimate ends and responsibility remains deceptive here, and threatens to make of itself too much. Even an ethics of responsibility does not attain to the fullness of Weber's word, to what is thought in *disenchantment,* nor properly to the way in which the vision of the last men

---

[37] An excellent account of the way in which the truth of beings is revealed to biotechnology is given by Bradley Bryan, "Bioethics, Biotechnology, and Liberalism: Problematizing Risk, Consent, and Law," in Law Health Journal 11 (2003), 119-136.
[38] See Terry Maley, "Max Weber and the Iron Cage of Technology," in Bulletin of Science, Technology and Society 24:1 (Feb. 2004), 69-86, esp. 77. Maley's argument is, I think, particularly instructive here insofar as it can be read as belonging to a more familiar and insidious argument concerning "politicization" as redemptive from oppressive forces of late modern homogenizations, which one tends to find within all variety of "critical" works of research unable to break with the basic liberal problematic of the willful subject. C.f. especially, for instance, the works of Donna Haraway or Edward Said.
[39] Weber, "Politics as a Vocation," 127.

could show up as one of a naïve paucity. The passion with which he comes to think the figures of politician or the scientist stems not merely from an apprehension of aporetically irreconcilable value-spheres. Our reading is perhaps made harder by the fact that *one may indeed* find such a formulation within his work, that he does say: "a *mature* man . . . acts by following an ethic of responsibility and somewhere he reaches the point where he says: 'Here I stand; I can do no other.'"[40] But we should perhaps hardly be surprised if what is gathered in a thinking as rigorous and as expansive as Weber's is not reducible to the terms of rational formulae; one must attempt rather to inhabit that gathering than merely represent it, to sense what is most profoundly named therein.

And indeed: a recuperation of Weber as ethicist of responsibility hardly renders due to what continues to resonate most thoughtfully within his work, which gestures rather to a persistent sense of loss, of *emptiness* attendant to a technological culture, which would seem to confront us today as inundated precisely with a liberal concern for responsibility. As Nikolas Rose has aptly shown, for instance, one must understand the language of technical adjustment, management, and enhancement of selves which mark contemporary "advanced liberal" governmentalist logics as inhabiting a space of constant contestation and ethical/critical inquiry, concerned precisely with questions of risk and consequence – i.e., with ways of somehow assessing potential benefits and burdens of particular measures and technologies and of thereby working to engineer the conditions under which those benefits could be made available in an ethically informed way.[41] Indeed, it is precisely as a way of engaging an ethic of responsibility – understood in a way which seems formally identical to Weber's formulation, as a mindfulness of harm understood as consequence – that ethicists can turn today to ways of making risk associated with decision acceptable through the securing of consent. Such an ethics, it has been noted, must accept not only consent as an act of willful autonomy, but an assessment of risk which understands consequence in terms of technological truths about the nature of the world.[42]

---

[40] Ibid, 127.
[41] See Nikolas Rose, "The Politics of Life Itself" in Theory, Culture, & Society 18:6, esp. 9-10.
[42] See again Bryan, "Biotechnology, Bioethics, and Liberalism." An implicit ethic of democratic proceduralism would seem to reside here in the precise way in which responsibility comes to be routinized. Weber's own discussion of responsibility would seem to revolve rather around the possibility of the charismatic "politician", i.e., leader in some sense – which indeed has a certain

The very fact that Weber's heroic moment of political willfulness should thereby stand to be made available as part of a routinized managing *par excellence* of "concerns" about technology may be sufficient to render spurious the grandeur thereby connected to a mere formula. But further, we can see that an "ethics of responsibility", far from requiring any break with technological seeing, would seem rather to *perform the completeness and justness of that very seeing*. For this reason, an ethics of responsibility can serve to provide precisely an *impetus* to research, to laying bare the world in its causality that one may better gauge the consequences of one's decision. Working out such an ethics, one follows in principle from an understanding of what belongs properly to man as causal ground, reaffirming a project of *thinking from out of principle* as such so as to know in advance how to act; further, one proceeds precisely to enumerate the "consequences" of rationalization as what may be apprehended rationally (noted here as *violence* or *harm*) within a nexus of real causal relations. The implicit soteriological imperative of a secularized rationalization – that by ordering the world from out of the terms of intelligibility one may thereby render it somehow "best", "better", "more just", remains intact. An ethics of responsibility, then, would seem not only to belong to the way in which things come to show up as fungible, standing in relation to the will, but rather also to the way in which one might work to "invent happiness" as such – i.e., to guard through *cognizance* the very *obliviousness* of the last men themselves.

Call and Vocation

In this way, the iron cage would seem to house most convincingly its panther. A rigorous reason ensures that the integrity of its Möbius dance remains intact by insisting that the game of late modernity may be intelligently (that is, maturely) played. Indeed, it seems clear that we get no further insofar as we merely take from Weber the lesson of that obliviousness as a malignant *consequence* to be avoided, or mitigated as well as possible insofar as it follows *necessarily* from the terms of our thinking. Such questions already belong to the obliviousness of a management ethic itself, which at once poses and is justified precisely by questions of *efficiency*. And indeed: within a competitive context of increasing specialization, where the task of

---

historical connection to the very "threats" contemporary liberal ethics seems largely concerned to expiate (i.e., of coercion, of a meddling with bodies *unconsented to*, etc.). The central and modern metaphysical problematic of decision, however, remains the same.

thought falls to matters of research, where religiosity is recycled into the crowning glory and perfect compliment of a technological cult of *value*, in an economic and cultural context which demands the positive, the motivated, the cheap theodicies of feel-good ethics, and where an attendant irony offers just enough respite as to be reconciling – is it also not possible to soberly understand that it is indeed helpful and most prudent today to inhabit such obliviousness, and to be content in one's healthy entertainment?

Weber's work would seem, perhaps despite itself, to pose the image of the last man all the more uncomfortably to us: for he shows how life in the world today must *of necessity*, in the face of *irresistible force*, make its pact with management.[43] Shall we be surprised if life in the world today is indeed *easier* for one who assumes the vivaciousness of Kafka's panther, who is unmindful of anything lost in the dull banalizations of fungible commodification? We prefer, perhaps, to imagine that we had never rejected the world, as though we were only now, in our rediscovered and pacified leisure, coming to be faithful to it. But though we are furnished with all variety of noxious caricature (and the world of late capitalism would seem to specialize *par excellence* in the production of such caricature), the question is surely made too easy for us if we cannot also hear with pressing anxiety the question: what else is one to do? Where the question of value rings forth in the ordering of all things, what is to befall the unappealing? Finding too appalling the devastations of industrial development and the domination of nature, one works hard to make that nature banal, available as a resource for tourism. In such a context of rationalized competition as ours, it may indeed be upon pain of ruin, and the logging of the last tree, that one hesitates in taking up the mantra of "invented happiness".

Nonetheless, we suggest, it is also Weber who renders that mantra disquieting, whose thought bears the tension of one who *cannot* simply be reduced to an ethics of responsibility. It is precisely in his mournfulness at the flight of the gods, a residual sense of loss in march of reason, that *disenchantment* is revealed as an experience and

---

[43] This cognizance of a sense of irresistible force is an aspect of Weber's thought we shall attempt to further elaborate in the following pages. Evidence of his brooding upon such a question may be found at least as early as <u>The Protestant Ethic</u>: "The Puritan wanted to work in a calling; we are forced to do so. For when asceticism was carried out of the monastic cells into everyday life, it did its part in building the tremendous cosmos of the modern economic order. This order is now bound to the technical and economic conditions of machine production which today determine the lives of all the individuals who are born into this mechanism, not only those directly concerned with economic acquisition, with irresistible force." (181)

assumes its proper character. As we will show in our following chapters, rationalization belongs to a revealing of the world from which the living divinities withdraw, in which they appear precisely as marks of a "naïvety", an "enchantment". The modern project cannot bring forward that enchantment, but it does render it pallid, shunted aside (for instance) into a private sphere of "religious" values and experience. The experience of disenchantment, nonetheless, reveals that development precisely as the *flight* of the gods, as loss, and it is in keeping with this sense that rationalization is disclosed as *eviscerating*. In disenchantment, one intuits an experience of a different calling, akin to that of the prophet or the hermit: alone in the desert of reason, one fasts that one may ask after the gods in their beckoning. Such an experience *renders hollow any mere ethics of responsibility.*

In a certain sense, disenchantment might appear as nostalgia, as a resentful longing for what is past and is resolutely other. And indeed: this is how Weber's own account would seem to develop, through *sociological* studies of ancient Judaism, India, China. What was not like today's capitalism, and how did *they* live? But it is also clear that, while Weber's sociologies (as we will show) keep most markedly their *distance* from those worlds not disenchanted, neither are they *resolved* to that distance. Enchantment is neither something to be made available as presence (i.e., produced or reproduced), nor consigned to otherness (as museum pieces, available as marked *absence*); what is striking in Weber, and implicit within disenchantment *as such*, is rather that it resounds already from out of a curious kind of presence, which is itself precisely *in its withdrawal*. The experience of disenchantment would seem to come on its own as a calling; it is that call which, as it is heard by Weber, draws one to seek out after the gods, finding that they continue to speak *in some sense* from out of the character of what is, that the claim of their justice may still resound for us in some way. An attunement to that speaking and a mindfulness of its flight before a vengeful reason reveals the weight of an inexorable and impossible tension within contemporary existence: though one seeks to render due to what beckons from out of our dwelling, one must unavoidably take up the charge of resentment against it. That resentment stakes its irresistible claim because it belongs to the very way in which things show up today *as* calculable in connection with a thinking which is continually self-refining, self-scrutinizing; the question of *efficiency*, once posed, proves staunchly immovable and impossible to ignore, *for one gets no more efficient than efficiency*. Neither would a kind of messianic unification of divinity and rational lawfulness seem possible here: in Weber, as we will show, the very nature of the call would seem to forbid it.[44]

If Weber nonetheless could defend so passionately the figure of the politician, it is because that figure evinces an attempt to merge the discordant calls of thought and vocation, a remembrance of the gods and rational decision. As we will argue in Chapter 3, in Weber that attempt shows itself to be inevitably failed; it is an attempt to bring together which only reveals more clearly an essential dissonance. But one may yet wonder whether that tension does not become *all the more pronounced* today, as reason sinks ever more deeply into its uncanny slumber, as the memory of the departed fades before more lively reveries.

To simply reclaim Weber as a theorist of responsibility today would seem, therefore, to pass over precisely this tension, just as to ask the questions of management or of rational ethics ("Very well: but how shall we better order things?", "How do we rethink how we are in the world?", "How can a sense of loss help us escape our predicament?" etc.) immediately renders irrelevant and evanescent what can nonetheless strike with the force of disenchantment and draw forth our thinking.[45] It is to the experience of disenchantment in Weber, therefore, and its connection with a central questioning concerning the affirmation and rejection of the world – that is, as we have suggested, with a kind of *dike*[46] – that we now turn. It is only within the

---

[44] In this way, we think, the work of Giorgio Agamben, for instance, bears a marked departure from the thinking of technology and the "task" of thought as it shows up in Weber and Heidegger, who seem to me to be much more in affinity as regards their sense of "the gods", by whose departure the modern world is marked. See especially Giorgio Agamben, The Time That Remains: A Commentary on the Letter to the Romans trans. by Patricia Dailey (Stanford University Press, 2005).

[45] We should note, indeed, that even Deleuze's attempt to think ethics, as a call "not to be unworthy of what happens to us," would seem to retain a commitment to the rationalizing project of *working out in advance what one should do in a way which is true always and everywhere*. This by elaborating formally on the "whatness" of what "happens", i.e., as steeped in virtualities, in such a way as to draw us out in preparation for worthiness by grasping properly "difference", "sense", etc., as a *concept*. That concept may show up as something to be *lived*, ie,. as a path whereby we are drawn into the shattering experience of the "eternal return"; but this would seem, however, to remain in a certain way a kind of "Dionysian" messianism, which seeks to bring the rapturous into proximity with the mundane under the sign of a self-conscious productivity. See, for instance, Gilles Deleuze, The Logic of Sense trans. by Mark Lester, ed. By Constantin V. Boundas (New York: Columbia, 1990), esp. 149.

[46] We might note that our aim in invoking *dike* here is *not* to engage a discussion concerning the most accurate definition of the term or to make any sort of scholarly claims concerning its precise meaning for "ancient Greece" (which, in any case, would require a much different mode of approach). We speak, rather, of the experience of disenchantment as "connected with a *kind* of *dike*" – not to render disenchantment identical to *dike* but to try, in bringing the terms into resonance with one another, to articulate something central to the character of Weber's "call". For *dike* seems in some sense highly apt here, though it also gains in the constellation of our thinking a distinct character, which develops and belongs most properly within that context. We think *dike* here as connected with a call to "do justice", to "render due", which must be thought to show up, to arrive in the way almost of a visitation

context of such questions – and thus with an understanding of Weber as hunger artist – that we may come to know the sense of his vocational lectures and methodological work, and the experience of the "call" we may glimpse therein.

---

and which bears the character of an injunction. Moreover, the thought of *dike* here is intended to resound less with the harmonies of Plato than with an attempt to glimpse an experience of the world as roamed by gods – one recalls that, for instance in Homer, there is a sense of reverence, of paying heed to the struggling divinities attendant to the way in which one might "know" *dike*. To be drawn by the call of *dike* in this sense seems inextricable from an attempt to take seriously that struggle and that world. It should also be clear that the call of *dike* as it is thought here appears as something that is obscured by that very mode of rational thinking which from the beginning ensures the disappearance of the gods. What is suggested is not that Weber is "god-fearing" in the sense that Odysseus might have been, or that he might become so, nor that he might "have" *dike* or that doing so might constitute any kind of redemption, resolution, promise; rather we merely find it suitable to try to think Weber's listening-away after gods in connection with a kind of search to do justice to them, to render them their due even in their withdrawal.

Chapter II

Neither asceticism nor contemplation affirms the world as such.

The product of the potter, the weaver, turner and carpenter is much less affected by unpredictable natural events . . . The resulting rationalization and intellectualization parallel the loss of the immediate relationship to the palpable and vital realities of nature . . . This provokes the rationalist quest for the transcendental meaning of existence, a search that always leads to religious speculation. Ecstatic frenzy or dreaming are replaced by the paler forms of contemplative mysticism and of common-sense contemplation.

-Max Weber, *Economy and Society*[47]

What is to be said, then, of disenchantment? It may be that, like that call by which the prophet or visionary is seized, so too is disenchantment a voice heard only by *some*, who may only turn towards what already beckons. Weber, after all, saw that thoughts – and most markedly, thoughts of special significance – come "to" us, in their own time, and not "from" us as something we own.[48] Perhaps one must already have sensed how a life governed by rationalization could show up as a "polar night of icy darkness and hardness", under a reigning spirit of asceticism and rejection. But we must attempt nonetheless to see what is gathered in "disenchantment", and what is the nature of that call – and this not merely because it reveals more fully Weber's own work and lends to its more adequate representation. Certainly, his writing thereby gains clarity, as does his position within a trajectory of thinking which develops, I would suggest, in particular through Nietzsche to Heidegger. But through disenchantment we may also follow Weber to his most difficult thinking; it is here that he expresses the character and fullness of existence as it could show itself to him and as he could meditate upon it, that he might seek to "affirm" it.

As a call, disenchantment *comes* – it confronts us in its arrival in a way which *shows up our rationalized existence in some sense as hollow, as impoverished*. Weber spoke passionately of a search to "find and obey the

---
[47] Weber, Economy and Society, 548, 1178.
[48] See Weber, "Science as a Vocation," 136.

demon who holds the fibers of [one's] very life" – is this the light in which we are to think the nature of that confrontation, as a divine illumination which reveals itself upon the way, through long and hard toil, from out of a kind of faithfulness?[49] Such a confrontation encounters a sense of the divine as a presence; we are no doubt familiar with the way in which such a showing must bring with it a sense of an *expansion* of vision, before which our thinking hitherto feels small. But such a language, of abundance and paucity, threatens to be misleading insofar as it recalls only the language of Christianity or of post-Platonic philosophy and their subsequent intertwinings. For disenchantment bears, I think, a significantly different character, which rather forces our thought out in questioning: how could the world show itself to a thinking which had *not* already rejected the world? What has been given up?

In such a questioning, thought would seem forced out into an abyss; nonetheless, within such an abyss we would seem to find ourselves only more thoroughly where we already are. For implicit here is also another question, which lies silent within Weber's posing of the first: rationality renders the world empty; what also then belongs to what presences? It is in this way that Weber's text threatens to be misleading: his sociologies on the one hand inquire into *what is gone* in the sense of *actual relations and arrangements* which one can see to in some way have passed, within a continuum of *things that happen* within a measured (historical) flow of time. His studies of those arrangements, as we will see, retain always a distance – the experience of a world not "rationalized" in the Western sense remains irreducibly *other* to his explanatory descriptions of it. On the other hand, it is clear that the path of Weber's thinking is marked by an imperative to pay heed to what speaks from out of the "past", to in some sense glimpse it "empathetically" – i.e., to attempt a leap out beyond what is granted by the terms of rationality; that leap preserves in its presence and *as* presence the shadows of tradition, of gods, of prophecy.

One encounters here as "abundance", therefore, less a vision of something like the sublime – which might draw us nearer to redemption (a crucified Dionysus), or appear as a preparation for reason's heroic

---

[49] Ibid, 156.

(redemptive) coming into its own (as in Kant) – than the intuitions of a much more stern and bitter (if grander) expanse. Not even predominantly Dionysus, but the more treacherous and chilling wind of a world roamed by *gods* is intuited here. Their presence, if not what it "was" (one says no longer, or with the same sobriety, "Let not the gods not bring such a thing about!"), seems nonetheless to haunt the earth, scant of speech and immaterial like the very shadows of the Homeric dead.

As we have seen, Weber remains faithful to the experience of dissonance and tension which attends that godly vision, and to its specific character in an age of ascetic rationalization and eviscerating resentment. Just as the whisper of the gods leads one to *prepare*, to *seek out after them*, to render them their due, so do we glimpse with bitterness an *impossibility* encountered within that gesture, an inevitable and continual betrayal of one's sense of what is, made necessary by life in the world today. Seeking the gods is tinged resolutely with a note of failure (such belongs, indeed, to the character of that seeking, its continually silent or preparatory work amongst *shadows*): not *contradiction*, but *betrayal*. But that betrayal would seem to reach its height in the happy relegation of the gods into the realm of the *religious* as such, of belief, *for it is precisely intellectualism which grants the separation of value spheres*. The beckoning gods rather demand not to be confused with the imperatives of management (the scientist is no prophet), nor privatized – though, as the iron cage asserts itself ever anew this would seem all too often to be their lot. In Weber, rather, one glimpses the same tension and the same relentless sobriety with which Heidegger, who nonetheless thought so often about the Greek gods, could write:

> As though it were still possible for that essential relation to the whole of beings in which man is placed by the technological exercise of his will to find a separate abode in some side-structure which would offer more than a temporary escape into those self deceptions among which we must also count the flight to the Greek gods![50]

In what follows, then, we shall pursue the course of Weber's thinking on disenchantment more closely, so as to make clearer its character, its tension

---

[50] Heidegger, "What Are Poets For?", 114.

and its calling. We shall attempt to show in disenchantment a *fundamental questioning concerning the affirmation and negation of the world*, where "affirmation" must be such that it cannot come merely from the rendering of a judgment. This questioning will be shown to develop in conjunction with an analysis of specifically Western forms of rationality and rationalization, and their attendant expiations, which is evinced most clearly in Weber's comparative sociological studies of religion. In this way, we will come to reflect more fully upon the experience of disenchantment, which belongs to our technological era but which seeks out beyond its terms, and which brings with it the seeds of inevitable tension.

Rational Rejection

As we have suggested, the question of the affirmation and negation of the world runs throughout Weber's work, both as a central theme and as a deep compulsion within it. Like Nietzsche, Weber could see within Western rationality a primal moment of negation, a seething No against "the world". His work, at one level, depicts *sociologically* the story of Nietzsche's Great Crime: thus the history of Western rationalization is the story of the development of a constructive re-ordering of social relations, economic and political life, the development of formal law and bureaucratic specialization over and against a set of arrangements *historically* prior – e.g., substantive law, personal bonds of allegiance, a fuller sense of cultivated humanity typified by the Confucian "gentleman", and so forth. But the *resentment* of Western reason comes not from the way in which it "makes possible" the supplanting merely of one set of social arrangements by another; rather it resides within the character of that "rational re-ordering" as such. Western, constructive rationalization, for Weber, is granted from out of the way in which rational *thought* takes shape, is predicated upon a specific and unique form of *parting against what shows itself*, of mastering it, of *subduing* its dangers through a particular mode of *securing* oneself against them. One is reminded of the words of Lucretius, for whom an apprehension of the *truth* of things already evinces its rootedness in *an effort to expunge terror*, to make more *benign* what is, and to turn the worlds of gods and demons into fantastical and erroneous causal assertions: "Fear holds dominion over mortality/ Only because, seeing in land and sky/ So much the cause whereof no wise they know,/ Men think Divinities are working there."[51]

In this way, Weber proceeds to distinguish Western reason's implicit project of *correction* from "other" forms of "rationality" not so concerned (for Weber, something like a rationality may develop in a variety of contexts and with differing natures). Thus he writes: "The effect of the *ratio*, especially of a teleological deduction of practical postulates, is in some way, and often very strongly, noticeable among all religious ethics."[52] In Confucianism, for instance, Weber finds a highly developed bureaucratic rationality which was nonetheless quite different from that of the West: while the Confucian official discharged his function within a routinized and hierarchically differentiated system of administration, his was a rationality which never broke with the powers of tradition. Confucianism demanded a rigorous self-control oriented towards the demands of a sober practicality – which Weber calls a kind of "utilitarianism", but which took shape as a turning of energies, an adjustment to the cosmic forces of the Tao whose nature granted the possibility of harmonic balance. Such was a rationality governed throughout by an ethic of *adjustment to the world*, rooted in an esteem for conventional propriety. Thus, the Confucian "wished neither salvation from life, which was affirmed, nor salvation from the social world, which was accepted as given. He thought of prudently mastering the opportunities of this world through self-control."[53] The administration of the state was not articulated in opposition to, nor was it in the end separable from, the intercourse with spirits in an enchanted world, which took the form of "sacred ceremonies, the magical efficacy of which had been tested since time immemorial, and in the form of sacred duties towards the ancestral spirits."[54]

---

[51] Titus Lucretius Carus, De Rerum Natura (On the Nature of Things), Book I, trans. by William Ellery Leonard, available at: < http://classics.mit.edu/Carus/nature_things.1.i.html> (June 4, 2007)
[52] Weber, "Religious Rejections of the World and Their Directions," 324.
[53] Max Weber, The Religion of China: Taoism and Confucianism trans. by Hans C. Gerth (New York: MacMillan, 1964), 156. As such, Weber works to show how Confucianism and its ethic of world-affirmation could grant developments point by point differentiated from the modern West: the presence of substantive (rather than formal-legalistic) justice, no rational money system or bookkeeping, an absence of logic and calculation as concerns for thought, the ideal of the cultured gentleman rather than the specialized official, prudent self-control to the end of "keeping face" rather than the Puritan's ethical rationalization towards "definitely qualified conduct" through self-mastery of one's own nature – to name only a few examples. See also 125-7, 149, 242, 244-5.
[54] Ibid, 148. The above discussion is also garnered from 226-249. Weber also notes that magic, though itself intensely "rationalized" and often if regarded "skeptically" by some of the literati, remained a central force of life in this world – such that its eradication would have been *practically* impossible. Disasters political and natural signified the offense of spirits and the neglect of duty on the part of the

Weber's work traces the question of the affirmation and negation of the world through a variety of contexts, on the one hand attempting to analyze those crucial developments which could lead to the rationalizations of modern technological culture, and on the other describing those worlds marked by a thinking and organization resolutely other to our own, which precisely *could not* produce the rationalizations of Western capitalism. His analysis comes to focus on "religion", which here expresses at once a *fundamental thinking concerning the nature of what is*, an inquiry into the character of being, and a mode of attunement towards it. Weber could inquire into what "level of rationalization a religion represents"[55] because he was concerned predominantly with how varieties of doctrine and ritual could articulate and turn towards what showed itself – i.e., how religion reflected structures of thinking, which revealed a mode of comportment towards the world thereby disclosed. Religion becomes particularly significant here in showing up ethics of *salvation* – that is, in evincing most clearly and vehemently a spirit of *resentment* and *rejection*. Weber's investigations work at once to show a fundamental connection between modern forms of rationalization and the soteriological imperatives which take shape in relation to particular articulations of God, world and man; but they also point to how a thinking of how life in the world could take shape in the absence of such a soteriology, and what such thinking could articulate as belonging to being.

Thus, while Weber will on the one hand speak of "types" of rationality (thus Puritanism, in contrast to Confucianism, "represents the polar opposite type of rational dealing with the world,"[56]) he will also speak of "levels" (e.g., the "level of rationalization a religion represents"). A language of quality (where the category already seems somewhat spurious – hence the *effect* of the *ratio* being *noticeable*) suddenly becomes one of quantity; this latter arrangement evinces a deeper and pervasive concern with an analysis of the "rejection" of the world: how far has a religion gone in its hatred? The scale tips always unfavourably towards the modern Occident and its precedents; even the Hindu ascetic or the Jain, for whom suicide represents the culminative religious act, does not go so far as to *disenchant* and systematically *reorder* the world in a manner so pervasive and so devastating. It is the modern, and the Puritan "active ascetic" with which he is entwined, who permits

---

Emperor. "In China," Weber notes, "the belief in magic was part of the constitutional foundation of sovereign power." (200)
[55] Ibid, 226.
[56] Ibid, 238.

neither magic nor "fluidity" of doctrine, whose divinity lies most distant and is sought through *correct judgment*, clear before the intellect, and not through *gnosis*, demanding not merely an *emptying* but a *purification*.[57]

The "disenchantment" which characterizes modern life itself has many precedents; indeed, some form of disenchantment has characterized Occidental culture "for millennia".[58] For Weber, disenchantment is tied to processes of intellectualization, and the demand of the intellectual that the world should submit to the stamp of pervasive and unifying meaning.[59] Such "meaning" does not refer, however, to such articulations of the "eternal orders of the world" as Weber found in the *Tao*, which could articulate a sense of what forces one must engage and by what path one sought to live well *without* seeking redemption. What Confucianism lacked was rather "a unified way of life flowing from some central and autonomous value position,"[60] an apprehension of life as a totality in such a way as to *render judgment upon it* – i.e., to think being from out of questions of ethical *knowledge*, that one might then seek *redemption* in accordance with its dictates – i.e., correct it. Weber, following Nietzsche, can thus see in Christianity a debasement of existence (in a way which can then come to *actively* reorder it) before an elevated, supramundane, deified vision of truth.[61] Furthermore, the very nature of that truth would seem already to seek redemption and to stand in irrevocable tension with the "magical garden" of the world in *thinking from out of a lawfulness grounded in non-contradiction*. Weber notes, "The very concept of logic remained absolutely alien to Chinese philosophy" – that is, to a thinking which *did not already seek salvation*.[62]

---

[57] It is necessary to assert that there are a number of nuances to this argument which would nonetheless prove too great a divergence from our task to treat here. The central distinction, in Weber's treatment, lies between an experience of the godhead which is likened more to an "ecstatic feeling", a mode of contemplation which is always poorly described in relation to the language of the conceptual as we understand it, and one which may be sought precisely down the road of conceptual thought itself, providing a model and an anchor for it. The broad reference is to Max Weber, The Religion of India: The Sociology of Hinduism and Buddhism trans. and ed. By Hans H. Gerth and Don Martindale (Glencoe: Free Press, 1958).
[58] Weber, "Science as a Vocation," 139.
[59] Weber, Economy and Society, 506.
[60] Weber, The Religion of China, 232.
[61] Which spirit of nihilistic debasement remains and indeed would seem to deepen, in Weber as in Nietzsche, through modern developments of the subject as unified (or, we may suppose, subsequently schizoid) "personality", through science as account of the "real", etc. C.f. Friedrich Nietzsche, "How the 'Real World' at last Became a Myth: History of an Error," in Twilight of the Idols/The Anti-Christ trans. by R.J. Hollingdale (New York: Penguin, 1968), 40-1.
[62] Ibid, 127. The relationship of logic to a soteriology is also suggested in Weber's Ancient Judaism, where the concept of divine law represented an early approach to the *ratio* of later thought, but which

What marks so crucially the "disenchanting" force of Western reason, for Weber, becomes the way in which such a truth, granted from out of a lawfulness transparent to itself, can come to aspire *to bear upon things in the general case* in such a way as to enable its *constructive reordering*. Ancient Judaism did not reject or thoroughly disenchant the world because, though it was an ethical religion grounded in the notion of lawfulness by *pact*, that lawfulness could not come to bear upon the world or existence as a whole, for it was always *"this" berith* with Yahwe – who at the early time of the war confederacy was only *one* god amongst many – which brought the law to apply to *"this"* people.[63] In a similar way, early Judaism could not inspire the development of the "personality" in the sense of the Puritan because the conduct of the individual was not scrutinized as a unified whole so as to find within it *proof* of God's grace – i.e., that the totality of one's actions (which become precisely actions systematically unified within a totality) should exhibit the mark of *ethical correctness*. Nor could Yahwe's law aspire to apply universally, for Judaism retained always a separation between the God's chosen people and the *goyim*. Furthermore Judaism retained a highly *ritualistic* orientation, and thus could not inspire a properly *active* rationalization. It is rather with the advent of a properly *abstract* thinking, which could not only presume (as a metaphysical thinking of truth of things) that identity (and thus non-contradiction) belongs to being, but which could bear formally upon the general case, that Western rationality could become properly *systematizing*.

Notably, it is this (especially Roman) formulation of identity ("every A is itself the same") which Heidegger would come to find as the kernel of that technical thinking by which beings show up as fungible before the will[64], which Weber points to as the condition by which a "formation of rational concepts" proper could, in rejecting the world, come to *reorder* it generally, eviscerating the world by reducing it to its implicitly soteriological terms.[65] It is also this kernel which, as we have noted,

---

retained its specific application in the Covenant, and so its "lawfulness" did not until much later provide a language with which to think existence as a whole.

[63] The only exception here being only some late developments in Pharisaic Judaism, in which one can find such zeal for law as to render possible conceptions of God himself "studying" timelessly valid law. This enabled the development of a kind of "systematic thought detached from the single case" which anticipated in a certain sense the properly "constructive" rationality of Roman juristic thought, and thus the bureaucratic systematizations of modernity. Weber supposed that rabbinical ritualism was detained in this trajectory by, amongst other things, the pariah-duality of Jewish ethics, the practical-ethical rationality and "common sense" orientation of the early rabbis. See Max Weber, <u>Ancient Judaism</u> trans. by Hans H. Gerth and Don Martindale (Glencoe: The Free Press, 1952), 414-5.

[64] See especially Martin Heidegger, <u>Identity and Difference</u>, 23-35.

[65] C.f. Max Weber, "Bureaucracy," in <u>From Max Weber</u>, esp. 218; Weber, <u>Ancient Judaism</u>, 414-5.

sets what we have termed the "call" of disenchantment resolutely apart from any effort to work out (in advance) how "instrumental rationality" may be redeemed through reason's contemplation of ends, whether "ultimate" or "responsible". This is so because to feel the weight of disenchantment is also to glimpse what belongs to it *as* an "impoverishment", and thus to seek out beyond it; whereas to work out in this way an "ethics" is predicated precisely upon such a metaphysical and systematizing thinking, and resides as internal within its terms, presuming precisely the principle of identity itself. For it is only within such a thinking that one may in any way come to such a project for thought (i.e., to work out in the abstract what may be done because man and his actions stand to be thought in the abstract), or any of its constituent parts – e.g., willfulness as the causal activity of the self, decision bearing upon the contingent, the mode of demarcation of instrumental from ethical reason, and so forth.

This rational thinking, further, is for Weber the "decisive" factor which, amongst other things, enabled bureaucracy to develop in its distinctly Western form (and most purely in the *modern* era), through the routinization of behaviour so as to render it *calculable* – i.e., that it should come increasingly involve the formal and impersonal discharge of duties by officials specialized in particular *functions*. Such bureaucratization provided the administrative and organizational context correlate to the Puritan asceticism by means of which one came to fabricate of oneself a unified "personality" which found ethical fulfillment in the adoption of rational conduct.[66] It is the Puritans who, marrying the energies of an intense salvation ethic oriented solely to the terms of judgment itself (lacking, for instance, the quietistic contemplation still found in Luther) with the vocational demands of a rationalized vocation, could usher into being a rationalization so totalizing as to be unprecedented in the scope of its evisceration. Thus, Weber notes: "Nowhere has the complete disenchantment of the world been carried through with greater consistency."[67]

The specifically religious motivations which Weber saw as necessary for that unification may well have faded before more mundane variants. But that salvation ethic, even if no longer phrased in connection with a supramundane God, is nonetheless implicitly retained within that rationalized life and thinking which, in

---

[66] See the later Introduction to Weber's The Protestant Ethic, 26. It is also telling that the very bureaucratizing forces which "de-personalize" (i.e., formalize) the work of (now specialized) officals are those which grant the (precisely "impersonal") "personality" of modern man capable of managing himself.
[67] Ibid, 226.

retaining *logic* and that *metaphysical* thinking which grants it at its core, parts resolutely against the world and disenchants it. Thus while no mention is required of the Puritans in Weber's formal expression of disenchantment – that is, that "one may in principle master all things by calculation,"[68] – one nonetheless finds that same spirit of asceticism within it, implicit within the way things can show up as calculable, and thus as *fungible* and as *resource* for the willful subject.

World and Affirmation

We have seen, then, how that Western rationality which disenchants could show up as a "rejection" of the world. But in what sense is "the world" thought here, such that one may seek in some way to affirm it? For if Weber shows what belongs to "disenchantment" as evisceration, it is also true that his thought evinces a searching-out after what is thereby lost. Weber may have proclaimed himself "religiously unmusical" (particularly, one gathers, in relation to those "arms of the old churches" opened wide[69]); but this is so because his work evinces a kind of piety much less readily housed, because the call of *dike* is heard in some sense from out of what is, resonant with *things* but also most strongly with what appears as lost, as echoes of a spectral past.

Weber says of the world: it is *irrational*.[70] But what is thought in this, it is clear, is not simply what one arrives at by presuming a "rational" world and then negating it. The world is "irrational" insofar as that saying predicated upon the metaphysical principles of logic must part in some sense against it in tension. One encounters, in this way, a strange duplicity: on the one hand, *the world "is" disenchanted*, things *show up* for us as fungible, we *are* in some sense subjects; on the other, that fungibility is always almost an illusion, a vague sort of ruse, an impoverishment.

This duplicity inheres throughout Weber's *sociological* studies: from his work in *Economy and Society* to his more focused studies, phenomena are described in a language of ideal-types, and a language of "actors", who have "interests" and experience various "states". A familiar (Kantian) world of subjects and objects comes into view; but at the same time that account continually points beyond itself and

---

[68] Weber, "Science as a Vocation," 139.
[69] Ibid, 155.
[70] See, for instance, Weber, The Religion of China, 227.

shows itself as poor. Whereas Weber will, on the one hand, study a world not "disenchanted" through its dissection into approximations of abstract variables, he will also, on the other, indicate how that thinking continually falls short: whereas we speak of geography, religion, rationality, structures of worldly rule, we are also brought to see that such abstractive thought is itself strange to the worlds we are attempting to glimpse. Chinese thought develops in connection with *this* agricultural cycle and *this* rule, with *these* spirits.[71] The aim and the truly difficult task is precisely *not* to see how we all offer varying *representations* of things, or do (the same) things *differently*; it is to ask after the world of the Confucian, and to see how his world *is that world*. And moreover: it is to pay heed to that world *as it yet speaks*. Again, in the case of magic: as a kind of "primitive rationalism", it is at once a kind of calculation and yet having to do with the presence of "incalculable forces" even though, as his discussion of magic in *Economy and Society* makes clear, our sense of calculability is awkward in relation to magic which "follows rules of experience," but is "not necessarily in accordance with a means-end schema."[72] The word of the Confucian sage is a kind of aesthetic "end in itself," although it is clear that such terms are out of place here.[73] Grasping fungibility as the mark of disenchantment, one strives to go beyond it in order to attempt to inhabit in some way "enchanted" thought. Thus we encounter at once a constellation of metaphysics-negativity (we *can* paint these worlds *sociologically*, but the enchanted world is *alien* to that thinking), as well as an attempt to leap away from metaphysics, an asking-out after a world not so eviscerated, which does not lack clarity, but possesses it in a different sense. The hunger artist makes a show of lack, of absence, of breakages; but that gesture of lack is already one which also *preserves*.

What is expiated in modern rationalization and its precedents, and what vistas are glimpsed out away from its bounds? A lengthy list may be generated: for instance, capitalism eradicates sib power; disenchantment occurs in the systematic unification of "the relation between God and the world and therewith its own ethical relationship to the world;"[74] in divestiture from magic and ecstasy; and routinization stifles charisma. It is clear that, whereas such enumerations are effective in producing

---

[71] E.g., ibid, 20-2.
[72] Weber, Economy and Society, 400.
[73] Weber, Religion of China, 245.
[74] Weber, Religion of China, 226.

some picture of "enchanted" existence, they remain sociological building-blocks and one is pointed beyond them, towards a world which remains resolutely alien to such thinking. Weber's sociology, in accordance with the duplicity of its terms, on the one hand works precisely to name a set of *actual* relations or *states* which belonged to an "enchanted" world. The aim, however, is not simply to grasp such terms that they may be in some sense reproduced; rather one comes to see how the experience of the enchanted world remains quite other, how magic names not simply an erroneous causal understanding (though science will still take over "something" of it, enough that magic comes today to seem pale *as a means of producing effects*) but a different mode of being, a different attunement to "the world". On the one hand, then, that magic is gone, that life is gone, it can never be regained; on the other, what seems implicit, in light of Weber's thinking concerning the *affirmation and negation of the world*, is some sense that magic, not reducible to causal assertions, *also* gestures towards a very different sense and mode of being which *continues in some way to show itself*. In Weber's work, the character of what is revealed in this way takes shape in connection to a thinking of the divine; is it divinity, known in its nearness, as presence, which seems most gallingly expiated by modern rationalization, and it is this which the terms of a disenchanting reason must part resolutely against.

But what belongs to such an attunement to divinity? In particular, the nearness of the divine is thought in Weber in connection with an experience of ecstasy and with magic. Ecstasy here ought not, however, be reduced merely to accounts of it as a *state* of particular "religious" significance – such is precisely the language of those rationalized "theologies" which have turned away from the world. Not only does an apathetic-ecstatic possession of the godhead form the center of intellectualized Indian soteriologies, but Weber will say more generally: "theologies presuppose that certain subjective states and acts possess the quality of holiness."[75] Nor does his discussion esteem ecstasy merely as *transgression* (just as he will disdain Romantic flights into the irrational), but rather a certain organicism of ecstasy within experience as such, as belonging to the world *prior* to the drawing of lines in our habitual sense. Thus ecstatic experience tends to assume a centrality within religiosity which has not alienated from itself as distinct the realms of art (particularly important for Weber is music), of the erotic, or indeed of the political imperatives of

---

[75] Weber, "Science as a Vocation," 154.

violence and war.[76] Ecstasy suggests the charismatic presence of the supernatural within various permutations of the "professional necromancer" or "magician"; it comes as orgiastic and often ritualized intoxication to the layman, as the terrible nearness of the war-god to the beserker. Given Weber's later account of the separation of spheres in relation both to rationalization and the *anomie* of contemporary culture one may well be prepared to view such a narrative of loss as one of definite *decline*. But in the case of Roman rationalism he is explicit: in turning the Greek *ek-stasis* into *superstitio*, Roman Christianity came to view dance and music as unseemly, thus rendering it "infinitely poorer" than Hellenic culture.[77] Perhaps as *ek-stasis* is to *aletheia*, so *superstitio* is to *ratio*; its paucity comes from the eviscerating demands of the theoretical-intellectual, in bringing the law-giving principle of a ground to bear upon all things. But one may even find a certain esteem in Weber for the "aristocratic" virtuosi of ecstatic contemplation, even within the context of Indian theologies of world-rejection and salvation.[78] It is only that *contemplation as such* does not affirm the world; but Weber's thinking here seems not altogether dissimilar from that which saw the Olympian deities "let be" the old claims of the earth-deities and the reveler Dionysus which remained nonetheless separate in spirit: the realm of ecstasy and contemplation may call of its own right, but what does not follow is that rationalism which makes of it a vision of *salvation*.[79]

Magic as such receives an extended description only in *Economy and Society*. Like ecstasy, however, magic serves to express a kind of living presence of the divine in the world – but whose entirety nonetheless withdraws in some sense from the clarity of reason. While a kind of "primitive rationalism", it is clear that magic is neither emptied of the electricity inspired by the presence of the divine, nor it is overdetermined by a clearly systematized separation of world and deity. Everywhere here the strict drawing of lines after our habitual fashion is strikingly awkward, even

---

[76] See Weber, Economy and Society, 400.
[77] Ibid, 554.
[78] See, for instance, his comparison of the "intensive" thinking implicit in Buddhist teachings with the immediately "child-like" understandability of Jewish law, in Max Weber, Ancient Judaism trans. by Hans H. Gerth and Don Martindale (Glencoe: The Free Press, 1952), 397.
[79] Walter Otto, I think, offers an excellent discussion on this point. See Walter F. Otto, The Homeric Gods: The Spiritual Significance of Greek Religion trans. by Moses Hades (London: Thames and Hudson, 1954), esp. 158-9.

in relations between sacred and profane amongst the laity; Weber moves to a language of "dwelling" spirits, "possession," "incorporation."[80]

Weber's thinking demands that one work in all *seriousness* to see a world inhabited by spirits and gods, which takes shape in a leap away from thinking metaphysically, from residing within the special system of rules for reason's saying. That leap is thought in connection with an approach towards magic and to ecstasy, and also especially through a conversation with ancient China and (implicitly) Greece (in thinking through the relationships which developed between official doctrine and folk-belief in China, Weber cites Homeric Greece as the example "nearest at hand").[81] But whereas the (awkward) language of sociological science dominates Weber's text, and whereas we can see how the will and the "showing" of fungibility in some sense parts-against, that leap is attempted in near-silence *from out of what seems nearest*, from out of that thinking which must already "be there" but which is not so marked by parting. It is the prophet who has not known the complete departure of his god who "experiences all the abysses of the human heart."[82] But that nearness is not determined as proper to man in the sense of a faculty, even as the *ratio* of the *animal rationale*; rather it is precisely that form of intellectualism which most obscures it. For Weber, the experience of living divinity is in some sense thought in a most *intimate relation* to things as they may be revealed to one who lives *close to them*; this gains articulation in his passages concerning the loss of an "immediate relationship to the palpable and vital realities of nature", in his discussions concerning the development of "bourgeois rationalism" (which always entails the withdrawal of gods), in the way the divine appears close in a certain sense to both the warrior and the farmer, who may both face what unfolds in presencing with astonishment.[83] Divinity is neither allocated to self-conscious subjects nor to objects here (which must include "nature" as such, in the sense of what one preserves and manages as parks); nor may it be

---

[80] Weber, Economy and Society, 402.
[81] Weber, Religion of China, 175.
[82] Weber, Ancient Judaism, 273.
[83] The relevant passages here are, in particular, Weber, Economy and Society, 1178; and Ancient Judaism, 128-9, 206-7, 382. It is true that much of Weber's language concerning "what unfolds in presencing" is discussed in terms of "incalculable processes" or in the terms of an *unfolding of events* in the sense of a trajectory of *things that happen*. The difficulty with this language is that, in consonance with how we have already the structure of his text, Weber uses a language overburdened with metaphysical thinking and connotations in order to gesture towards something quite other to it. It is in an effort to flesh out in some way what is thought in that gesture that we have put to use terms which invoke a quite different, if more Heideggarian, sense: the two thinkers, as should be clear from our discussion, may (we suggest) be brought together into an intriguing consonance.

thought in accordance with the rules of abstract identity (those things that are divine are so always and everywhere). One is rather charged to see how a god *may* show himself in a sense more intimate than what is open to such thinking, to those who have not grown deaf to such calling.

Weber may well, in his sociologies, counterpose "traditionalism" and "active rationalism" (i.e., it is the power of the sib which capitalism must have broken), but one nonetheless sees within his thinking a certain traditionalism of his own. This should not be understood in the sense of simply *representing* the sociological structures of traditionalistic cultures and what belongs to them (though, indeed, his sociologies do accomplish this), or as an attempt to bring back what may be so represented. Nor does Weber attempt merely to be "traditionalistic" about contemporary rationalized life. Rather, in his thought we see an attempt to approach those worlds not as chronologically distant happenings, but rather from out of that thinking which is nearest as bearing in some way upon it, that they may in some sense prevail in the mindfulness of what is present.

It is clear that the world, to one who seeks out the gods in this way, reveals within itself a startling nature: for where the guard of Lucretius or of Christianity grows weak, the world grows sterner. Not simply Dionysus or even the ritual of the Eternal Return's impossible redemption awaits; rather one intuits the draft of which Walter F. Otto offers apt description:

> Here is a more biting wind: everything great is dangerous and may confound the man who is not on his guard. In the realm of the gods there abides danger . . . they are themselves the danger. Often they crash into the well-ordered life of man like a storm. . . Here only vigilance and strength avail.[84]

A less benign world, and more treacherous; the gods who roam here grant no moralizing and no lasting security, but neither any gnawing guilt which follows from the blame taught by the doctrine of the will. The nobility of the adventurer, and not the palliation of fear, attends to the reverence of such gods.

For Weber, it is along that road kept by the gods that the way is opened by which death is more somberly approached and allowed to resonate as death, as what most ominously and completely lays claim to man. This is because the reign of

---

[84] Otto, The Homeric Gods, 246-7.

technology renders silent the call of death, turning it rather into what simply lacks meaning, what cannot be thought or adequately encountered within the progressive language of management and science, within the thinking of value.[85] Nietzsche could still think death as cessation in relation to the will, that is, to what is made secure as the principle of ongoing and self-overcoming processes of *life*, ("What does not kill me makes me makes me stronger,"), which thinking continues to dominate (for instance) in the writings of René Girard, who could later and forebodingly articulate death as having sacrificial *value*.[86] Weber's thinking, however, reveals an inadequacy and an inevitable distancing within such accounts, because they ask already what death (like all the world) can be within the clarified terms of knowledge, and so do not encounter and inhabit death, nakedly, as what pervades and closes the being of mortals. It is this which grants a certain "satiety" to Abraham or to the peasant, who completes in death the full cycle of his life.

The affirmation of the world, in this way, is thought along the very road which brings us most near to death, as to the abyssal and biting plenitude of being. "Affirmation", though implicit throughout Weber's thinking, never receives direct treatment in his works, which is consistent in keeping with the hunger artistry of his text, which always takes shape as a technological language glaringly inadequate, as a presencing of lack. For affirmation, as should be clear, may precisely not be thought here as a judgment, a Yes against the No of reason; rather it takes shape as what calls to thought, as what is approached in thinking what is most near, in the awed questioning of existence, as the beckoning *dike* of the gods.

As divinity, known in its nearness, recedes before rationalization and the salvation theologies of the West, so too does the world: as one draws nearer to disenchantment, in all Weber's writings, it is the gods who depart. Such is the implicit movement of his sociologies of religion, of *Economy and Society*, of *The Protestant Ethic*. And though the deity of Occidental theologians enters into the terms of our instrumental rationality, even He resides there only as a husk. Heidegger has said, in a similar spirit: "Man can neither pray nor sacrifice to this god. . . man can neither fall to his knees in awe nor can he play music and dance before this god."[87] To reduce

---

[85] See Weber, "Science as a Vocation," 140; and "Religious Rejections of the World and Their Directions," 356.
[86] See Nietzsche, The Twilight of the Idols/ The Anti-Christ, 23; and René Girard, Violence and the Sacred trans. by Patrick Gregory (Baltimore: John Hopkins University Press, 1979).
[87] Heidegger, "Identity and Difference," 72.

being to the stamp of meaning, to that which can be made clear before thought on the basis of systematized criteria of what such clarity can mean, shows itself here as a radical killing, an *unfaithfulness* towards the awful abundance of being. Modern rationalization assumes a totalizing scope in its inner-worldly direction towards the rendering-calculable and thus manageable of all things. What technological thinking seems implicitly to promise – the invention of happiness for Nietzsche's Last Men – remains predicated for Weber upon the bad faith of a childishly "understandable" soteriology lacking in nobility and awe.

Loss and Memory

We have nonetheless suggested that to encounter the call of disenchantment is in some sense *flattening*, that it bears with it an irresolvable tension and a sense of loss. The beckoning of the gods instills here a searching, a preparation, an asking-out after the world and its affirmation. But that seeking brings with it the character of *failure*, for one seeks to render due to gods that only *withdraw*, and one is left to feel always the weight of their abandonment. Weber's thought always rounds on itself with bitterness: we are not pagans; that world is gone. One seeks in some way to build from out of what is nearest, to live in some sense "naturalistically", which is the mark of those worlds which seem now "enchanted". For that is what marks the thought and life of ancient China and Judaism: a certain "naturalness" in one's relation to wealth, to sex, to the necessities of political prudence – in the sense of not having in the first place rejected, let alone *rediscovered* them.[88] Wealth is a mark of being favoured by the gods, but is not *proof* of a judgment of grace; spells, in turn, could be employed to bring favour in the market. The constructive-juristic rationalization of economic and political life had not yet forced the articulation (unfolding through processes of definition) of the religious as belonging properly to its own (today private) value-sphere, nor has "the religious" come to reside in the purely non-instrumental or the irrational, nor as the moment of "faith" in the selection of values.

For Weber, to live today is to unavoidably take up the active rationalization (and thus rejection) of the world; we are irresistibly forced into the iron cage of the

---

[88] see, for instance, Weber, Ancient Judaism, 400-4.

ascetic subject as the condition of survival in our everyday world.[89] This is so not only because things do show up as fungible; but because one is *forced* inexorably, within a context which shows up as properly *competitive*, to actively advance that logic of rationalization on pain of ruin – for it is this logic which governs the development of our modern world as such. The bureaucratic management of a calculable world, formal and impersonal, has shown itself to be "practically indestructible", far superior in its *efficiency* than any competing mode of life.[90] Weber himself, in his inaugural Freiburg lecture and as an officer in the German military, saw the value of rationalizing processes in the context of competitive struggles necessary within the world, and in his involvement in World War One personally fought for effective bureaucratization of the military hospital which was his charge.[91] "The Puritan wanted to work in a calling; today we are forced to do so,"[92] – this claim bears no less upon one who should attempt to flee it in the mere rejection or negation of economic or political life.

And indeed, as the officer of Imperial Germany, Weber would seem to have only condescension for those who "cannot bear the fate of the times like a man"[93]; for in affirming the world one must also face up to the demands of life in its seriousness. Those very sociologies which reveal an asking after world and god focus primarily upon orthodoxies – i.e., upon those religions which have not broken with the more stringent demands of worldly life, principally the imperatives of war and questions of rule. Similarly, the figure of the prophet, whose absence within the modern world Weber mourns in his later writing, figures in his work on Judaism as a kind of middling figure, who may bring at least the rapturous presence of the divine will to bear upon affairs of the day.[94] Weber's thought is caught between an attempt to live

---

[89] Weber, The Protestant Ethic, 181.
[90] Weber, Economy and Society, 987.
[91] See Max Weber, "The Nation and Economic Policy," in Weber: Political Writings (Cambridge University Press, 1994) and H.H. Gerth and C. Wright Mills, "A Biographical View," in From Max Weber, 22.
[92] Weber, The Protestant Ethic, 181.
[93] Weber, "Science as a Vocation," 155.
[94] Weber's mourning of the prophetlessness of his day is brought out in "Science as a Vocation," esp. 153. The prophet of *Ancient Judaism*, as a kind of rationalism predicated upon the scrutability of the divine will, resides somewhere between the early ecstatics and later Rabbinical legalism (the nearness of the divine, in its torturous visitations and passionate discharge in prophecy, sat uneasily with the latter). (Ancient Judaism, 291, 273, 412) It has also been suggested that Weber himself entertained certain feelings of identification with the figure of the prophet, particularly Jeremiah, though in the end he knew he was no such man. Indeed, such a figure was, as he has repeatedly stressed, nonexistent in his day, and certainly could not reside within either of the vocational spheres in which Weber applied himself – in politics and in scholarship. See Gerth and Mills, "A Biographical View," 27-8.

up to the world he inhabits while aware that its annulment is the condition of such engagement.

Sheldon S. Wolin has written that Weber's melancholy at the disenchantment of the world "issues from the frustration of a consciousness that knows that its deepest values are owed to religion but that its vocational commitments are to the enemy."[95] But it is rather precisely the question of *value* itself which is here most onerous: for where "religion" merely occupies a sphere, a set of values, one remains oblivious precisely to the way in which "religious rejections of the world" are already at work in that rationalization by which "value" and "sphere" may take shape as such. Indeed, Weber suggests nowhere that the capacity for "religious" experience has been lost to us. The flight of the mystic is always open to those gifted for it; a kind of genuineness of religiosity may also be found to reside, he suggests, *pianissimo* within our most private circles.[96] But even this, just as art *qua* art, appear only as residues of a living religiosity churning round in inoffensive eddies granted by the unavoidable current of things. Thus, he can write: "what is hard for modern man, and especially for the younger generation, is to measure up to *workaday* existence."[97] What has been lost is the living "*pneuma*, which in former times swept through the great communities, welding them together" – and which has withdrawn in the development of value-spheres.[98] As a man of the orthodoxy, Weber mourns the irretrievable loss of the gods, expressing an affirmation of the seriousness and fullness of existence.

To feel the weight of disenchantment, thus, is to inhabit unavoidably a site of tension, where one is caught, on the one hand, by the demands of the day, by the necessity (if not the moralism) attendant to the injunctions of technology – indeed where one must already inhabit the position of the willful subject in being called to effect accomplishments, to act in the real world, to make changes, to predict and make plans. On the other, that thinking comes to evince an emptiness, an ineffaceable distance, which nullifies continually any effort to pay heed to what is disavowed – that is, to any attempt to glimpse "what" is nearest, to meditate most intimately upon

---

[95] Sheldon S. Wolin, "Max Weber: Legitimation, Method, and the Politics of Theory," in The Barbarism of Reason, 305.
[96] Weber, "Science as a Vocation," 155. But we can also recall Heidegger's words here, in which we hear the echo of Weber's melancholy: "The loss of the gods is so far from excluding religiosity that rather only through that loss is the relation to the gods changed into mere 'religious experience'." See Martin Heidegger, "The Age of World Picture," in The Question Concerning Technology and Other Essays, 117.
[97] Ibid, 149.
[98] Ibid, 155.

being and upon death, to hear the echoes of gods. That tension and that rupture is shown to mark fundamentally our era, in which things come to appear as calculable; and indeed, it takes shape only in relation to that unfolding by which the world comes to be rationalized as such. But neither does that disavowal attendant to technical thinking remain open to one called by disenchantment, who remains drawn by what comes to assume precisely the character of the *inconsequential* once the question of efficiency has been posed, and which must remain *private*.

Within such a context, it is perhaps not surprising that Weber should have become a scholar concerned to detail what must have been expiated by technological culture, and moreover to make of that detailing precisely a hunger artistry which gestures to that very expansion of vision by which the "disenchanted" seems impoverished. But it is also true that Weber continues to feel most gallingly the injunctions of *vocation*, of willful *production*, of the *necessity* of assuming a *position*. Though what is disclosed in disenchantment takes shape as inconsequential, and so cannot be confused with that planning which brings consequence, it is clear that this disclosure remains torturous, that disenchantment arrives as a seeking-out of the *gods*, a call to build from out of what is nearest. But it is here that Weber, caught in some sense within the moralism of the will, evinces an attempt to *make of disenchantment something consequential*, to *enact* in some sense a remembrance of the gods, that it may *inform the practice of vocation*, the *rendering of decision*.

It is to this attempt, at work within Weber's vocational lectures, that we now turn. In this way, the passion of Weber's defense of the politician and the scientist serves all the more to show up precisely the fundamental *ruptures* of his thought, from which arises the enraptured impossibility of that very gesture.

Chapter III

> "*Many old gods ascend from their graves; they are disenchanted and hence take the form of impersonal forces. They struggle to gain power over our lives and again they resume their eternal struggle with one another....*
>
> *... So long as life remains immanent and is interpreted in its own terms, it knows only of an unceasing struggle of these gods with one another. Or speaking directly, the ultimately possible attitudes toward life are irreconcilable, and hence their struggle can never be brought to a final conclusion. Thus is necessary to make a decisive choice.*"
>
> -Max Weber, *Science as a Vocation*[99]

We have seen how Weber's thought bears the traces of an inevitably failed search for the gods, asking implicitly what it might mean to experience the presence of living deities, and attempting to come to terms with the stakes of their departure. His questioning makes the matter difficult for us – for it becomes clear that even to leap away from that metaphysical thinking by which things are made calculable does not mitigate its claims upon us, nor does one thereby escape the impoverishments of our era. This is why we must come back always to melancholy, to a thought of brokenness and disjuncture and expiations. His writing rather hurls back at us the hard lesson of the unavoidable betrayal of being's terrible *fantasia*: for we are forced into the iron cage of the ascetic subject as the condition of survival in our everyday world, which force becomes all the more galling for one called upon to *decide* and yet already defeated in doing so.[100]

We have observed technical thinking undertake all manner of strange recyclings so as to perform the completeness of its seeing. But one might also say: does not Weber undertake his own recycling, enacting a rediscovery of struggle, of ecstasy, of polytheism itself, bringing into proximity with his modern world that which has so clearly been lost? Does not a certain inspiritedness reside, for Weber, within the "personality" of vocational man in his devotion to the demon who holds fast "the fibers of his very life," and which acts as a kind of counterforce to the

---

[99] Weber, "Science as a Vocation," 149, 152.
[100] Weber, The Protestant Ethic, 181.

eviscerations of instrumental rationality?[101] Despite his own admonitions against the "romantic irrationalism" of his day, there would nonetheless seem to inhere within his work a certain residue of the Romantic, which shows itself in a rediscovery of polytheism insofar as these are brought precisely into relation with the subject and its knowledge. Figures of myth are revived as expressions of ontological principle or as inhabiting the spaces granted by it; one finds recurrent within Weber's vocational and methodological writings a turn to the imagery of the gods, to the frenzies of inspiration and a dance with the infinite. But how are we to understand these gestures? Somehow, one must be able to act today, to take up one's vocation – does Weber merely render palatable that which already must be done? Does he merely redeem a technological life by making it colourful?

Such a question would seem to bring us back to questions concerning the quasi-redemptory possibilities for "resistance" in Weber's vocational lectures in particular – such as is often discussed in the interpretive literature and by those committed thereby to a defense or reiteration of liberalism. Does Weber simply run the circuits of a Kantian project, invoking reason as the judge of reason, working out what may be done, and what hoped today? Our suggestion has been that Weber is no such reconciled ethicist, that his thought evinces rather a different theme. For the call of disenchantment already renders poor such a project, and brings to clarity how any such recovery of the gods into the realm of the consequential must fail. Furthermore, to take Weber as merely working-out a problematic of decision does not take stock of the *character* of his defense of the politician and the scientist, of what is gathered into the passion of those portrayals.

We have suggested, rather, that the moment of decision in Weber's texts attempts to enact in some sense the impossible, to bring together the divergent calls of disenchantment and vocation, to bring forward into the life of the world that vision which came in the desert. Feeling the moralizing injunction of the will, Weber attempts in some sense to *enact* a remembrance of the gods. The aim of this chapter will be to inquire into this "enactment" and its character.

Weber does indeed, as we shall see, bring the gods into relation with the will in a kind of recycled polytheism, thinking them from out of those sites of creativity familiar within modern accounts of the subject and state politics. But no less do we

---

[101] Weber, "Science as a Vocation," 156.

see within that attempt a continual doubling of thought upon itself, which simultaneously enacts a remembrance and feels the pangs of betrayal and failure. Inspecting closely the healthy figure of vocational man, one glimpses instead the gaunt double of the hunger artist, who makes a show of lack and withdraws into a haunting silence. It is this doubling which lends Weber's texts their passion. And it is in this way that the vocational moment of decision can assume less the quality of reconciliation or of any kind of "solution" arrived at than an impossible and grand moment taking unto itself the weight of an age, an enraptured pronouncement which has passed already through the graveyard of all hopes. Thus, for instance, Weber can write, at the end of *Politics as a Vocation*:

> Certainly all historical experience confirms the truth – that man would not have attained the possible unless time and again he had reached out for the impossible... And even those who are neither leaders nor heroes must arm themselves with that steadfastness of heart which can brave even the crumbling of all hopes. . . . Only he who in the face of all this can say "In spite of it all!" has the calling for politics.[102]

Such impossible moments of the will are not unfamiliar within the trajectory of German thought within which Weber was situated. Kant's categorical imperative sought at once the unprecedented enactment of moral action purely from duty as what nonetheless belongs most properly to our nature, and which bore the character of man's awed imagining of the universal – that is, of man's humble approach towards God.[103] Nietzsche's overman could similarly affirm the thought of the Eternal Return, a figure whose redeeming character has its birth in a vision which flattens all hope of redemption. But whereas the Kantian moment continued to seek God down the road of reason, approached by way of imagining what could bear without contradiction upon the universal as lawfulness, and whereas Nietzsche could invoke rather a frenzied tumultuousness in which the thought of the universal precisely denies such a *harmonized* vision, the character of Weber's passion seems different. Not only would Weber seem to lack the polemical fervour granted by a metaphysical securing of the will to power as the principle of life itself; rather the "grand moment" of his thinking here stems *not* from an encounter with the will as the condition of "faithfulness

---

[102] Weber, "Politics as a Vocation," 128.
[103] See especially Immanuel Kant, Groundwork for the Metaphysics of Morals, 2nd Edition, trans. by Lewis White Beck (New Jersey: Prentice-Hall, 1997), 23, 54-9.

towards the earth" in Zarathustra's sense, but from precisely the *irreconcilability* of that faithfulness with life in the world which "enforces" willfulness as its condition. It is a moment, therefore, of the *melancholic* will, which seems almost already too wise for what it attempts, and for whom that irreconcilability remains unendingly torturous, brought out ever anew as one feels continually the demand of the historiographical *moment* which calls for *action*.

We shall inquire, then, into that doubling within Weber's vocational lectures, into his enacted remembrance and disenchanted withdrawal in the figures of the politician and the scientist. In this way we shall attempt not merely to mouth the formulae of those lectures' contents – which repeat familiar themes of "freedom", of politics, of the creative force of the "new" within willful decision – but rather we must come to these things in following the *path* of what is thought therein, which we have traced in the way disenchantment comes as a call, drawing thought out beyond an abyss: that is, we must allow the emptiness Weber reveals to resonate, we must pay heed to his *melancholy*.

The Wheel of History

It is perhaps not surprising, in the face of a continual brooding on the obstinate inexorability of rationalization, that one finds within Weber's writings a persistent concern with what forces might break in some sense with routine, with the calculable. A set of oppositions recurs throughout Weber's work between rationalization and what appears (within the technical language of his text) as the breach of the incalculable, which is described (though often awkwardly) in connection with a kind of "creative" force and a nearness of the divine. Once again, however, one encounters an unavoidable sense of disjuncture; though the contemporary politician and the prophet are discussed in terms of an opposition between "charisma" and ordered economy, in is clear within the context of Weber's work that one cannot conflate a modern problematic of decision or of "newness" with the nearness of Yahwe, or with a "naïve" experience of political life.

That naivety takes shape as other to modern, rationalized political life; but it is also thought in some sense in connection with it. Just as presence of divinity is thought in connection with a nearness to the world and its dangerousness, so too is political life as an engagement with imperatives of rule and war, with violence.

Weber's persistent concern with orthodoxies, as we have seen, reflects this sense: those who remain faithful to the world, who do not seek salvation, also have not broken with politics. As the divine seems near to the farmer close to the "vital realities of nature", so too does it smile upon the warrior. Thus the nearness of Yahwe the war god or the god of the prophets (for whom the divine will bore directly upon the affairs of the day) stands opposed to the later consistency of pacified priestly law which sees the withdrawal of the divine. In a similar way, for Weber to draw near to the gods is to draw near to their *struggle*, and to that *dangerous* "fate" which holds sway over that struggle.[104] In some sense, it is the warrior who is held out in the biting wind of that fate, into the uncertain and violent currents of worldly change, which may turn suddenly to show the favour and nearness (or indeed the wrath) of a god.[105] Those who could feel that wind, and partake in that struggle with all seriousness, would seem to have been closer to that awed questioning of existence which may see the emergence of new and living "religious" thought, which "presupposes the capacity to be astonished about the course of events."[106] Such questioning stands precisely apart from the secure "chatter" of intellectuals doing research or offering up "religious feelings" as a topic for discussion; this questioning rather lies closer to the poet, to dreamers and knowers of ecstasies.[107]

---

[104] See Weber, "Science as a Vocation," 148.

[105] As we have suggested, this is largely the movement charted in Weber's Ancient Judaism, in which one passes from the nearness of Yahwe as war-god, known as rapturous presence in the charismatic frenzy of warriors, towards the systematization and rendering-consistent of Rabbinical law anchored to the *ratio* of the covenant (later occasionally elevated amongst the bourgeois Pharisaic brotherhood to the status of timeless law). Further, with this transition one sees a shift in the character of Yahwe from being one god amongst many, and at that a mighty god of the astonishing and the terrifying, of the whims of "irrational fate", whose warlike essence grew out of an association with the catastrophic-creative powers of mysterious nature, towards a god of wise order, granting an (in principle) comprehensible law and ethics. See Weber, Ancient Judaism, esp. 75-94, 128-9, 243, 415. In the Indian context, the implications of removal from the exigencies of political rule and warfare are rendered visible in the development of Jainism, which took to near-unparalleled heights the rejection of the world through a rationalism of non-violence. This did not amount to a distancing from divinity *per se*, in particular as seen in Jewish law nor in the mode of Puritan asceticism which sought salvation on the intellectualizing model of correct judgment. Jainism remained oriented towards the apathetic-ecstatic and non-conceptual experience of an impersonal godhead which lay open to man in the here and now. But this experience of the divine was also given shape by a metaphysical dualism of peace and turbulence, *atman* and *maya*, which grounded an ethics of *ahimsa* for which Weber nonetheless exhibits a certain disinterest. Thus, he writes, "Only a trader could truly practice *ahimsa*." (Weber, The Religion of India, 200.)

[106] Weber, Ancient Judaism, 207.

[107] Compare Weber, Economy and Society, 516, 1178; Ancient Judaism, 226. This is not to undermine the sense in which, for Weber, Yahwism was precisely not a cult *derived* from orgiasticism, but rather was oriented in its most essential aspects towards a rational ethics of action rooted in Yahwe's *berith* with his chosen people. For remarkable here is not the *absence* of orgiasticism, of ecstasies and frenzy in the Yahwist cult (particularly in its earliest days and to those who experience the divine presence

In the notion of "fate", one glimpses precisely the irretrievable experience of a living "politics" which has not already been made to disappear through the disenchantment of the world, and those rationalizations of politics which have seen efficient and routinized economies of violence take shape from out of a modern (epistemological) problem of foundations, of definition and distinction in the sense we have known since Hobbes. It is closer, rather, to the world of Machiavelli's paganism, which could see within the cycles of war and rule the perilous courting of Fortuna. But one sees here once again a movement we have charted in slightly different contexts: of *disappearance* as technique comes to hold sway over being, which enforces a continual backing-away from things in their nearness, thinking them rather from out of the clarified terms of a reasoned knowledge, which thinking is revealed to be as *devastating* as it is *effective* and *cannibalistically inclusive*. For such modern modes of thinking politics technically (as having to do with the willful decision of ends within the metaphysical terms of modern sovereignty, its modes of drawing borders, authoring laws, of articulating a reasoned economy of norm and exception – which can only take shape from out of a prior orientation to lawfulness) nevertheless take over in some sense the question of politics and the way it is lived. This occurs in the same way that the question of efficiency can "disqualify" magic as an "instrumentality" and render it vaguely unthinkable. But this "taking over" remains nonetheless implicitly soteriological, and *rejecting* of that earlier politics; a reasoned security already chokes out Machiavelli's dance with Fortuna.

Fate would seem nonetheless to be of persistent concern to Weber in his meditations upon the demands of vocation today. For it is clear that he attempts to bring a sense of the "struggling gods" into the terms of vocation – that is, into relation with the activity of the will and the problematic of decision as it gains articulation in state sovereignty. Even here, he insists that fate, and "not science", holds sway over these struggles – even though, as we have seen, fate would seem already to disappear where action in the world attains the character of *willing*, and all the more so as that willing comes to bear in principle upon the totality of things made calculable. For to bring the gods within the will as struggling values is already too much: as is made clear in Weber's thought on disenchantment, to secure before oneself the will as

---

most directly – such as the early warriors and the prophets), but rather the reverence of that ecstasy not simply for its own sake, but in its relation to the divine will bearing upon conduct in the world.

cause, before which things stand as calculable, must precisely and from the beginning part against the gods.

Identity belongs to being: as beings that will, we know already who to blame; as Augustine saw, to pose the terms of the will offers precisely a means of disqualifying the gods, which can now appear not only as false causal assertions but as an irresponsible displacement of blame (because the gods brought this deed about, I cannot have done so or be made to answer for it). One no longer finds in the dangers of the world a god to be revered; one seeks to expunge that danger, to localize it, coming to resent it with a gnawing guilt. Even Weber's somewhat Lutheran inflection of the will (that thoughts come to us of their own time, not from us as something we own), which would seem to allow a certain space for the struggling gods, already sees only and most markedly their withdrawal. For here the question of fate comes to be thought in relation to what man may "put his hand on the wheel of history"[108] – fate appears awkwardly as bearing upon that willfulness which brings things about, which effects consequences which may be tallied within the chronicles of counted (metaphysical) time.

Such a manoeuvre may hardly be surprising where we "are" in some sense unavoidably subjects, where things do show up as calculable, where one does inhabit modern history, with all its implications, in a very real sense. History – and the injunction to "guide" it, as well as the problematics of national and international politics which are implied in principle as what *enables* as well as *manages* that mode of "guiding" – seems to mark most obstinately the "fate of the times", which would seem to destine nothing less than the withdrawal of fate in a continual injunction to rationalization.

Nonetheless, it is clear that Weber *does* "bring forward" the gods to remembrance within his text, however awkwardly, and this is thought in connection with an opposition to a sense of the dreariness of routine and calculation. Just as "charisma", thought in connection with the modern politician, seems out of place and in some way distant from letting resonate the experience of the prophet, so too does the inverse appear to be the case. "Charisma", as gathering to thought an asking-out after prophets, seems just as awkward for describing the way one "does" politics today. What Weber attempts is to bring the two in some way into connection: just as

---

[108] Weber, "Politics as a Vocation," 115.

the presence of charisma could show up as the mark of divine election, the presence of "supernatural powers" by prophets and warrior heroes and the "opposite of all ordered economy," so might the charismatic politician bring forward something of that electricity into vocational life and rupture what seems stifling in a world which is calculable.[109] What is "rupturing" here already can hardly be expressed, transfiguring the gods into a language of the "incalculable", of the "new", brought into connection with willfulness; but what is sought, *as* what would seem to rupture and stand apart from that calculability, is rather in a kind of "bringing forward" of those intimations, those echoes of what does *not* enact already a backing-away, a disappearance of what is nearest. Charisma, thought from out of the call of disenchantment, bears the mark of the near made present in its nearness, as the revealed sign of the divine; Weber's "grand thought" resides within the wager that Luther's "Here I stand!" may resonate in some way with what *vanishes* before technique, with what seems more intimate than willfulness.

It also seems clear, however, that this attempt already bears the mark of failure – for one seeks to break out of what belongs most properly to vocation, whose terms remain nonetheless insistent. Not only would Weber, coming to give his vocational lectures *after* having written most of what now comprises his sociologies of religion, seem already too wise for such a wager – indeed, he makes clear that such a willful experience of gods remains precisely *disenchanted* (i.e., it too must in some sense show up as *empty*).[110] Moreover, such a remembrance, brought to bear upon action in the world *qua* guiding the wheel of history, has the character always of the *impossible endurance of the unendingly impoverished*: one attempts "*even that* which is possible today", within the "polar night" of the world, that long darkness of desolate winter.[111] The hunger artist would seem already to eclipse the politician.

Whereas a nearness to the violent winds of "fate" could bring with it an "awed questioning" loved by divinities, so does the chatter of professional intellectuals remain irrevocably removed from that awe; and Weber saw clearly that in the lecture-hall the prophet must remain silent, just as the prophet is distinct from the politician.

---

[109] Weber, "The Sociology of Charismatic Authority," in From Max Weber: Essays in Sociology, 245-8. The Gerth and Mills translation has been used for its eloquent succinctness in this phrase.
[110] See Weber, "Science as a Vocation," 148-9. What is accentuated is precisely that such "gods" today show up in a way which renders them already dead, "impersonal". Weber's phrasing reminds one aptly of Baudrillard: "Many old gods ascend from their graves; they are disenchanted and hence take the form of impersonal forces."
[111] Weber, "Politics as a Vocation," 128. Emphasis mine.

Indeed, so distant is the action of the politician from heeding adequately the *dike* of the gods, from in some sense building from out of what is nearest, that Weber must think the receding of the world's winter, even as relatively late in his thinking as his vocational lectures, as vague and distant, hardly to be thought. Elsewhere and earlier he could express that modern bureaucracy had become "practically indestructible", and that "history shows that wherever bureaucracy gained the upper hand, as in China, Egypt and, to a lesser extent, in the later Roman empire and Byzantium, it did not disappear again unless in the course of the total collapse of the supporting culture."[112] Escape from the iron cage appears only as the distant and cataclysmic abrogation of terms: this marks the final insistence of the cage as enclosing the totality of the real. Reason writes its own vision of apocalypse into history: not only do the gods grow silent as the condition of things becoming calculable; their "return" in any sense is deferred always to the borderlands of temporality, just as the sovereign state must familiarly defer "otherness" to the spatial margins.[113] And indeed: it is clear that any such final "undoing" of the iron cage takes shape precisely as other to what may be thought. Weber's methodology makes clear, in articulating a familiar (epistemological) constellation: where the reality of time takes shape as an endless line of homogeneous "moments" which "contain" in some sense the actualizations of *decision* and the play of efficient causality, one glimpses an endless expanse which effaces any sense of the cyclical or of fate. The ground is cleared for modern knowledge; and moreover, one imagines precisely that history goes on forever.

Where the call of disenchantment reveals of that history an endless wasteland, as far as one may see and with the hard insistence of the *real*, it is perhaps hardly to be surprising if Weber should attempt to remember the gods in those sites where "struggle" has been allocated by reason – i.e., within politics and within the creative otherness of the will. But no less does he come already too late to such remembrances, which galling sense of failure would seem always to settle as the last and melancholic word.

---

[112] Weber, Economy and Society, 1401.
[113] In this way, it is interesting to see that Weber's melancholic willfulness provides a kind of nightmarish double to Kant's sense of history: only here it is not cosmopolitanism which stands on the other side of a "magic moment", but rather the unthinkable undoing of the iron cage itself. C.f. Immanuel Kant, "Idea for a Universal History with a Cosmopolitan Purpose," in Kant: Political Writings ed. by H.S. Reiss (Cambridge: 2003), esp. 51-3.

Infinite Abundance

In *Science as a Vocation*, Weber discusses at some length the occurrence of ideas, which "occur to us when they please, not when it pleases us," as a gift of inspiration necessary for work in any vocation. Moreover, he writes:

> ... inspiration plays no less a role in science as in art. It is a childish notion to think that a mathematician attains any scientifically valuable results by sitting at his desk with a ruler, calculating machines or other mechanical means. The mathematical imagination of a Weierstrass is naturally quite differently oriented in meaning and result than is the imagination of an artist, and differs basically in quality. But the psychological processes do not differ. Both are frenzy (in the sense of Plato's 'mania') and 'inspiration'.[114]

The effect of this passage parallels Weber's discussion of charismatic passion in connection with the contemporary politician: "inspiration" stands to be thought precisely in relation to the vocational subject, in relation to the ascetic will rendered clear before itself and mustered towards work in a calling. The reference to "Plato's 'mania'" as describing "psychological processes" may seem strange within such a context, and from a thinker so nuanced; what seems emphasized, however, is the rootedness of Weber's discussion within a prior thinking oriented towards the delimitation of the real, of the science which knows it, of the subject who knows. As "psychological processes", inspiration and frenzy are observed here as the excited functioning of the mind held as object before itself, as bearing in a unified way upon the activity of thought as willfulness. Weber invokes a familiar and modern constellation in asking what excites the creative activity of the subject; the real stands already secured in order that inspiration may be thought in relation to its terms.

Weber's anachronistic reference to Plato is prefigured by his earlier methodological writings which lay out the conditions of that anachronism as historiographical social science. Just as we have seen history projected into the future as the homogeneous trajectory of the world's night, so does it here reach into the past: for his sociology presumes a naturalized metaphysics of willfulness, of individuals who have *motivations* and *values* we may attempt sympathetically to understand.[115]

---

[114] Weber, "Science as a Vocation," 136.
[115] See Weber, The Theory of Social and Economic Organization trans. by A.M. Henderson and Talcott Parsons (Illinois: The Free Press, 1947), esp. 91-99.

Similarly, it is in relation to such a metaphysics that Weber can delimit a specific relationship to a sense of "otherness" connected to "inspiration", which attains the character of the large and the expansive (similar to Kant's thought of the sublime) in relation to the activity and knowledge of the subject clarified before itself as finite. The "processes" Weber will later discuss in connection with "inspiration" gain clarity in his earlier writings as a dance with the infinite, in relation to the activity of the genius-scholar. [116]

The infinite here gains its character precisely and only through an epistemological inquiry which takes shape in relation to the self-clarification of consciousness as a "whatness" approached from out of the assertion that identity belongs to being. Proceeding from out of a prior orientation which gives to the truth of things the character of lawfulness thought metaphysically, one secures the finite synthetic unity of consciousness before itself, present before which stand the objects of its knowledge; demarcated as distinct from this may be counterposed (in Kantian fashion) a grandeur of experience present to a more passive "ego" and likewise an abundance to things. Such grandeur, nonetheless, remains thought in connection with those beings already present to knowledge. Thus the scholar actively and with desire *wrests* truth from the wealth and flow of things into representation with the aid of abstract "limiting concepts"; in a methodological variant of responsibility, this truth *confronts* an abundance (a kind of "reality") which is never reducible to it.[117] That abundance remains thought only as a kind of "other" to a reasoned truth, as a kind of excess; moreover, that excess is thought as a *plenitude of presence* thought in connection with phenomena (and, indeed, at times as the mere multiplication of what is "objective" in phenomena, as the "infinite causal web" of the real). Thus, Weber writes: "None of those systems of ideas, which are absolutely indispensable in the understanding of those segments of reality which are meaningful at a particular *moment*, can exhaust its infinite richness."[118] Time, as we have already seen, becomes

---

[116] See especially Max Weber, "Objectivity in Social Science and Social Policy," in The Methodology of the Social Sciences trans. and ed. by Edward A. Shik and Henry A. Finch (New York: The Free Press of Glencoe, 1949), 82.
[117] Ibid, 93, 104-5.
[118] Weber, "Objectivity in Social Science," 84, 105. Emphasis mine. But while everything would seem to hang upon the question of value, for Weber this by no means harms the possibility of a social scientific knowledge; rather, he seeks to lay out the condition by means of which, affirming the value of science as such, the will as relational centre of knowledge may undertake the necessary means to that end, positing limiting concepts and "constructing relationships which our imagination accepts as

projected precisely as an endless continuity of now-moments, each marked by struggle and abundance (thus, for instance, Weber can make reference to "the eternally onward flowing stream of culture").[119]

That very experience of infinite abundance projected into an endless flow of time similarly plays its part in that very ground-clearing by which we have seen cyclical time, fate, and the gods be made to disappear before the terms of technique. The infinite, as an abundance of presence which recedes from the active synthesis of the finite subject, belongs to the way in which each *moment* of all time bears the character of *struggle* which grants purely *contingent* meaning (thus "contingent" as against an eternity of homogeneous moments of struggle). The wealth and flow of things assumes the character of *intrinsically meaningless chaos* in relation to those beings which in some way "wrest" forth meaning. Meaninglessness becomes the negative presupposition for the active work of "what" is made secure as the relational centre of things – that is, the willfulness of man the producer.

In the articulation of the scholar as genius, a space is reserved for the dance of the finite thinker with the abundance of the infinite: as at once active and passive, in synthesis one also encounters what withdraws. And just as man grasps meaning from out of the "entirety" of what is given him, so is it in some sense "given" to man to understand what he does: Kant's aporetic tension between the autonomous will and the "purposiveness" of nature is carried forward in Weber's insistence upon the will's *passivity*: for thoughts come *to* us.

It is on the basis of Weber's articulation of this metaphysical position in his methodological writings, and within this "space" granted the experience of the "infinite", that Weber attempts his figurative remembrance of the gods in his vocational lectures (*figurative* because the gods, disenchanted, can now show up "as" only "impersonal forces"). Thus the gods "inspire": they beckon to us, holding man

---

plausibly motivated and hence as 'objectively possible' and which appear as *adequate* from a nomological standpoint." (92)

[119] Ibid, 104. In this connection, within the terms of Weber's sociological method, time and the notion of its infinite continuation would seem perfectly described in Heidegger's early discussion (and refutation) of Aristotle's understanding of time – where time becomes "what" is "counted" as a kind of now-moment which nonetheless points beyond itself within a horizon of "later" and "earlier" (i.e., time is thought from out of the terms of a knowledge directed upon extant beings which are present). Thus: "Each now has a transitionary character; each now is by its essential nature not-yet and no-longer. In whatever now I may wish to stop, I stand in a not-yet or a no-longer. . . If the nature of time is understood in this way, it follows that time must then be conceived as an endless sequence of nows. This endlessness is inferred purely deductively from the isolated concept of the now." See Martin Heidegger, The Basic Problems of Phenomenology trans. by Albert Hofstadter (Indiana University Press, 1982), 273.

fast by the "fibers of his very life."[120] But they do so in a way which, in Lutheran fashion, brings the otherness of revelation into continuity with the drawing-together as present of the self knowing itself as will.[121] The gods take up residence in the mysterious depths of the will's "otherness" and there churn in endless struggle; but the passion they grant remains such that it may be obeyed by means of *devotion to a cause*, i.e., by the positing of value (which must precede the articulation of truths).

Weber may suggest that the gods come to us in some sense out of things – thus that "we are placed into various life-spheres, each of which is governed by different laws"; or that "so long as life remains immanent and is interpreted in its own terms, it knows only of the unceasing struggle of these gods with one another."[122] Nonetheless, one remains rooted in a prior orientation to the will as what is in some sense most secure: as belonging to *value*-spheres, the gods belong already to a mustering under the sign of "this or that ultimate *weltanschauliche* position."[123] And for this world-view one must take responsibility in a manner which clarifies and (however aporetically) assumes ownership.[124]

Weber does articulate in his vocational and methodological works an understanding of "inspiration" and thus a kind of figurative proximity to the gods as they may be brought within modern frameworks of understanding. Again, however, the movement is the same: an impassioned attempt to make resonate with what seems nearest what one may do and articulate within vocational life – within a thinking

---

[120] Weber, "Science as a Vocation," 156.

[121] It is clear, in this connection, that Weber found Lutheran doctrine to lie in some sense apart from the ascetic fervour associated with Calvinism and Puritanism, insofar as predominant within Luther was an element of passivity whereby the experience of a calling as divine ordinance assumed a distinctively traditionalistic and contemplative air. See The Protestant Ethic, 83-7. For an articulation of the relevant discussion in Luther see Martin Luther, Martin Luther on the Bondage of the Will: A New Translation of De Servo Arbitrio (1525), Martin Luther's Reply to Erasmus of Rotterdam, trans. by J.I. Packer and O.R. Johnston. (London: J. Clarke, 1957), esp. Section 25.

[122] Weber, "Politics as a Vocation," 123; "Science as a Vocation," 152. Emphasis mine.

[123] Weber, "Science as a Vocation,' 151.

[124] The "religion" of the Homeric Greeks, which forms the image for the discussion of the gods in Weber's vocational lectures, must again be understood as utterly foreign to such a formulation which proceeds from a rendering-secure of man before himself in accordance with the dictates of a consistent and certain knowledge for which being serves as ground. Such an understanding of man derives, as Weber has shown, from a host of imperatives latently soteriological. One might draw comparison from the pages of Walter Otto, for whom the gods cannot be understood as derivatives of rationalism in this way but as taking shape in fidelity to man's dwelling, wherein one may sense in all happenings the image of the divine: "Whether the deed was good or evil, whether man may praise or blame himself for it, in no case can he believe that he brought it about himself, that he himself embodies a sovereign will whose goodness or evil is alone responsible for his acts and his derelictions. Transgression is no more condoned than its consequences are abrogated. But the feeling of wretchedness does not enter." (Homeric Gods, 175).

forcibly technical. Thus in *Science as a Vocation* Weber works to counterpose the scientist of true vocation, faithful to his "gifts" and who takes up his work with the whole of his being, with one not so intimately engaged:

> Now, whether we have scientific inspiration depends upon destinies that are hidden from us, and besides upon 'gifts'. Last but not least, because of this indubitable truth, a very understandable attitude has become popular, especially among youth, and has put them in the service of idols . . . these idols are 'personality' and 'personal experience.' Both are intimately connected, and the notion prevails that the latter constitutes the former and belongs to it. People belabour themselves in trying to 'experience' life – for that befits a personality, conscious of its rank and station. . . Formerly we called this 'experience,' in plain German, 'sensation'; and I believe that we then had a more adequate idea of what personality is and what it signifies. . . . only he who is devoted *solely* to the work at hand has 'personality'.[125]

The passage *echoes* the play of nearness and distance one encounters in Weber's thinking on disenchantment – the "personality" has passion, unerring *devotion*; whereas those "idolators" have *not even that sense of intimacy*, the condition of their engagement seems all the more removed, seeking out "experience" as something one "gets" because one infers from abstractions that one "should". A counterposition would seem to take shape between one who truly "lives" his vocation and his personality (which includes preparing for the visitation of inspiration through an ascetic *devotion* to one's work) and one who is merely the collector of himself, who is belaboured to have "experiences" and so reveals all the greater a distance from them.

That "echo" is redemptive in structure, opening the possibility of uniting bureaucratized existence through the "gift" of inspiration – unity of reasoned lawfulness and the breath of divinity, a kind of care for what recedes which amounts to a "fullness" of life. But we must see already that Weber comes to articulate that "resolution" from out of a thinking which knows all too well such manoeuvres, which can see already an impoverishment in such a rationalized reconciliation. He attempts rather an impossible actualization of *gods*, which impossibility has already been grasped in the *rejection* of the world implicit in such an abstract working-out, and which is emphasized in Weber's articulation of such actualizations as *disenchanted*. Any ethics thought in this way remains a properly *moral* (read: *soteriological*)

---

[125] Weber, "Science as a Vocation," 136-7.

undertaking, which presupposes a unifying account of one's self and one's conduct in order then to devoutly "live" it.[126]

If Weber's gamble is that such an "echo" of nearness, as what is "even possible" today, may accomplish the *impossible*, may enliven the pronounced deadness of rationalized existence in bringing to light what must thereby disappear, then that attempt seems no less tinged with failure than was its correlate in the realm of state politics. Such an attempt asks that the soteriological bring about in some way a "faithfulness" to the world, as though what may be attempted in this way were not so overwhelmingly a deformed echo, already too distant, already only a wintry desert.

Weber may indicate disdain for the person who "cannot bear the fate of the times like a man," who cannot get to work to meet the "demands of the day" – but we have seen that he comes to this question as part of a larger reflection bearing upon the affirmation of the world as such.[127] Seeing how what belongs to "workaday life" is precisely a parting-against "the world", Weber seems to display almost a desperation in attempting to resolve that obstinate tension, the panic of one who seeks inclusion where none may be had: surely, what draws thought most intimately, which lets speak not only divinities but death with its most ominous and isolating call, may in some way be consequential! Thus Weber may attempt even to *justify* a remembrance of the gods (as faithfulness to inspiration), in relation to *vocational requirements* – that is, to the *necessity* (efficacy) of such a remembrance in the production of ideas, in one's *success*. Such an account, however, would seem to mirror in a manner only more *mundane* the way in which the Puritan could seek *proof* of divine grace in his rational calling: for whereas the ascetic behaviour helpful for the attainment of wealth once *incidentally coincided* with the imperatives of divine judgment, now one hears almost a tone of desperation where even a figurative proximity to the divine (as dance with the infinite) is put forth as somehow *relevant*, somehow *valuable* to genuine vocational undertakings. The divine proves itself in our work.

But even that panic would seem to have grown old for Weber himself: such modes of inclusion must appear as already hideously soured, already steeped in *betrayal*, coming from one who could brood for so long upon the dependence of *precisely that thinking* upon a prior *rejection* of the world. As what excites the will, even the gods now appear in the mode of resource, known and valued in their effect:

---

[126] Ibid, 151-2.
[127] Ibid, 155-6.

and Weber himself has shown us how such a thinking can belong only to a time of ongoing and refined annihilation, to a world approaching the character of sport. It would seem clear, then, that what is unsettled in the very same passages by the call of disenchantment cannot by such "remembrances" be put to rest, nor that unsettling rendered its due. Such an implicit sense of failure lends passion to Weber's "impossible moment of the will"; but that moment comes precisely *in those very lectures* in which he shows so clearly at once an understanding of what is at stake in "doing science" and "doing politics" *and* a sense of the irrevocable disenchantment of our era. Indeed, Weber writes as one who knows *all too well* what is already implicit in his task as scientist, and in theorizing a life which seems somehow less abstract, less eviscerated, *from out of the very terms of that impoverishment itself*. His writing exhibits the tension of one who sees that he already inhabits the position of the will, and feels the *continual* weight of *each moment* as precisely the call of *history*, which demands remain *very real* – and yet is drawn all the while by another call, which shows up in that thinking a continual backing-away from what seems nearest, an ongoing disappearance of the world, of death, of things.

The Melancholic Will

Regardless of how Weber's reference to Plato's "mania" may have been "intended", that reference seems in the end entirely apt, despite the *anachronism* which unsettles its *accuracy*. For Plato's "mania", as *divine* ("*theios*") mania which shows up a mode of relation to gods, bears an essential continuity with "vocational" inspiration – which continuity is revealed in glimpsing rationalism from out of logic *as* a kind of cage, *as* disenchantment.[128] For both the *theios mania* and the will's inspiration inhabit an enclosure of thought away from the warring divinities of the world, in relation to which the gods appear as an expiated otherness, as it were across an unbridgeable gap. Indeed, even that most direct of Weber's meditations on disenchantment – which articulate its relation to the presuppositions of *logical* thought

---

[128] This is the term used, for instance, in the *Phaedrus*, in which the "possession" of inspiration is discussed in relation to love. Plato's treatment here enables a hierarchical arrangement of those "lovers" who are nearest to the gods as *having seen the most of the realm of Forms*, which places the philosopher and true lover at the top, and relegates the soothsayer and the poet down near the bottom, above only the farmer, the demagogue, the tyrant. See Plato, Phaedrus & Letters VII AND VIII trans. by Walter Hamilton (London: Penguin, 1973), esp. 50-55.

and bring us to articulate the principles of identity and of contradiction as conditioned by rejection – remains already only a *formal* contemplation, already distanced, already parting against what beckons in disenchantment. Weber's thought, as we have seen, must leap away from that metaphysical thinking in silence, gesturing towards what nonetheless seems nearest to our dwelling, which unfolds along the approach towards the whispers of once-living gods. Plato's discussion of inspiration draws us precisely to contemplate this moment in which the 'magical garden' of the world is transfigured under the light of reason, where the abyss appears out beyond which the gods and the poets who know them are flung.

Weber's excited willfulness resonates with that elusive moment of transfiguration in Plato whereby the poets (who, we know from the *Ion*, most "are" poets when they are inspired) come to be marked by a "childish passion" – in how the gods re-emerge in relation to the truth of the philosopher, oriented towards what is most purely in being without contradiction, towards "unity arrived at by a process of reason . . . which a god owes his divinity to dwelling upon."[129] In Plato, the poets are already "impious" insofar as they do not bring the gods under the light of *reason*, insofar as divinities are not eclipsed by truth: those who say the gods do battle are in error because the gods are *good*, and it is not consistent for what is *good* to do harm.[130] It is clear that Plato, belonging to the world of Greek antiquity, remains far apart from Weber's iron cage, even if we can see that his thought in some sense prepares the way for its development: but no less would that fundamental moment of the Socratic No seem to resonate, in drawing man away from the world towards the "reality" of reasoned truth. For Plato, the specters of banished gods would seem to linger as an unsettling presence, shadows of a disavowed past, whose return is to be warded away by the spells of argument: "we will still listen to [poesy], but while we

---

[129] Plato, Phaedrus, 55.
[130] One might further compare Plato, "The Republic," trans. by W.H.D. Rouse (New York: Signet Classic, 1999), 176-7 (378C-380A) with Walter Otto's reading of Ares' entanglement with Aphrodite in Homeric Gods, 243-6, which emphasizes how it was precisely a mark of the "naivety" of Homeric thought that it could see quarrelousness and cunning as belonging properly to the gods – only later rationalizing thought could see this as "disrespectful". It may perhaps be of further interest that Weber himself makes note of Plato's dismay at the Homeric account of the gods – as a "completely unrestrained relationship" which came to be understood as disrespectful. Perhaps Weber's only omission on this point is that he does not draw out the consequences within the context of this disjuncture; he claims only that disrespect for the gods could develop only removed from the cultural centers of the Greek religion, and does not ask how what was at one time essential to the character of the gods could later be translated into impiety. But such a questioning, I think, would not contradict, but rather follow from the general lines of his analysis of rationalization. See Weber, Economy and Society, 1284.

listen we will chant over to ourselves this argument of ours, this, our reasoned incantation, careful not to *fall again* into that childish passion. . ."[131] That incantation remains implicit in Weber's "enacted remembrance" – but no less does his thought also reveal a more perilous, a more silent path, which rather preserves as presence the spectral and terrible echoes of gods, and which could hear there a *beckoning* in which resounds the call of *dike*.

Well might that beckoning bring today a sight worth banishing: a graveyard vision, a desert where one is accustomed to see life, a skeletal frame of pronounced loss. Even Weber would seem to have found too desolate that horizon and yearned to enliven it; so much harder must be that expanse for one able to hear the persistence of Weber's lingering and whispered abjection, to see the grim smile of the hunger artist already too wise and too embittered. But that is nevertheless the path Weber discloses, which is at once the way of gods and of ghosts, which knows at once awed reverence and despair.

While one must follow in this way the hunger artist to learn what is gathered in Weber's torturous "moment of the will", that silent withdrawal is by no means necessary for the usual task of plumbing Weber's essays for an ethics. Unmindful of his melancholy, one is able to hear in him rather all our favourite and most tired catechisms: an orientation towards the valuating will as what is most secure, reason's insistence upon itself in confronting its devastations (and all manner of recycling thereby made necessary), a reiterated problematic of decision. One catches even hints of that cynical resistance we would seem to have learned so well, of one who sees the character of sport in everything and yet, with an undisturbed shrug of the shoulders, plays anyway, or plays ironically.

Weber writes: "Our civilization destines us to realize more clearly these struggles [of the "gods"] again, after our eyes have been blinded for a thousand years – blinded by the allegedly or presumably exclusive orientation towards the grandiose moral fervor of Christian ethics."[132] Like the entirety of the essay from which this passage is drawn, these words exhibit a doubled thought. Watching the unfolding of a world become sport, and glimpsing in his own vocational engagements the emerging primacy of the valuating will as the relational centre of all things, Weber suggests a projection of *things the will comes to bear upon through the course of technique's*

---

[131] Plato, "The Republic," (607C-609B) 408. Emphasis mine.
[132] Weber, "Science as a Vocation," 149.

ongoing refinement, a movement of the will towards the rediscovered liveliness which we have come to know so well. Weber could not see how the primacy of valuation could merge again precisely *with* new convolutions of Protestant Christianity as a dispelling of doubt, a renewed orientation towards the godlike righteousness of technological man. But he does outline the course of the *cognizant* will so often invoked against it, which remains no less oblivious in its approach towards completeness. And indeed: we are to realize *more clearly* the struggle of *values* – this much seems only confirmed by celebrations of Weber as *politicizing* knowledge, as one who pushes forward the *calling into question* of all things in a mode which prepares already for *decision*, which seeks (in principle) the invigorating excitement of politics in *everything*. As a projection of the will's *historical* movement, there would seem to be much here which rings *correct*.

But we sense here also another meaning: that this movement, which brings everything into relation with man and "his" civilization, should show up precisely *as* obliviousness – as blindness. Here is no happy *prediction* that "we" will somehow overcome together the iron cage – for we know all too well how such projections of *things that will happen* pan out as already historiographical, and how convincingly history reveals in itself an endless expanse. Rather, *experiencing* the call of disenchantment, one feels a tension with the realm of the consequential *grow* as one draws nearer along the trail of the fugitive gods. As the vision deepens the desert remains implacable yet seems more distant, more difficult to inhabit in any conventional sense; one is only *spurred on* by its emptiness, *realizing more clearly* what belongs to the struggle of the gods in sensing all the more our distance from them. *Our civilization destines us*, it compels in showing all the more pervasively its disavowal: the wasteland, for one drawn to see it, bears the character of *growing*, revealing implacably its deepening oblivion – woe to him that sees it! Learning the hard lessons from Weber's already-failed redemption, shall we be surprised if what resonates all the more is the way disenchantment *comes* in a way which is *flattening*, which kills action that has become already technical, which is consequential? Which renders all the more *torturous* and *hollow* those very ethical formulae Weber could still attempt to utter *and their subsequent refinements*, though we recognize them to remain as defensibly *necessary* and *effective*? Shall we be surprised, as life facing the serious "demands of the day" gains increasingly the character of pantherine entertainment – from which in the end one sees no escape – if the bitter smile of the hunger artist, who *can only fast*, should arrest us all the more resolutely?

Conclusion

Long is the destitute time of the world's night.

-Martin Heidegger, *What Are Poets For?*[133]

Less an ethicist, I think, than a hunger artist stares up at us from the pages of Max Weber's work. A gaunt frame is composed expertly in a gesture of lack. Revealed in that performance is a vision harrowingly stark: an endless winter marked on the one hand by disavowal and the oblivious impoverishment of Nietzsche's last ones, and on the other by an endless tension, the galling promise which sees the "demands of the day" revisit continuously the melancholic will. If Weber's attempt to bring together the divergent calls of thought and vocation was already failed – as it seems clear that it was – then no less is there disclosed therein and all the more unbridgeably a *fundamental divergence* which continues to mark our era, and from which one finds no resolution, unless it be in the utter oblivion of thought's call to reflect more intimately and more originally upon death and god, and in them upon the character of man's dwelling in being.

Weber could inhabit ethically the moment of decision in such a way that it tore him apart: but though we by no means escape its claims, the passion of that moment seems somehow faded, the terms of engagement all the less nourishing – what could once flare up enough to engulf him even for a moment seems now only a dull smouldering, grown for us too old to kindle much heat. Weber could still find some signs of life within the orthodox political life of his day but who today is able to see this, once a world of management and resource comes to resonate at all as impoverished, once one can draw the hard consequences of that impoverishment and not yearn merely to be reconciled through the old mechanisms of messianic rationalism? For we would seem to know all too well who today will "make a difference" – who will take part in politics, who will save the trees, the silenced, even the bored – and to know *how it will be done*, and *down what roads*. We know what work makes clear what has been lost so as to make it once more present and available,

---

[133] Heidegger, "What Are Poets For?" 90.

and we know what is invested in that effort. Moreover, we can see precisely how the experience of disenchantment comes in a way which *flattens* that work, and likewise how the disavowal of that experience can be neither surprising nor *indefensible*. But it nonetheless seems that the climb to the sovereign heights of decision is striking today less as something for which to strive than as that which has always unavoidably been done, an old routine which grows tired but with which we are nonetheless inundated.

But no less does Weber, throwing into relief the betrayal attendant to our technical age, draw us out towards the beckoning call of gods, preserving in the fullness of his vision what shadows remain, what echoes may yet stir. No *escape* from the iron cage and the endless expanse of metaphysical time is granted; but he does point us along the way which reveals more daringly what presences, and which brings one already to prepare, to approach in *seriousness* the memory of gods, to let them prevail in thinking which is not merely technical. Hearkening to Weber's word, one is drawn to let resonate that challenge, to glimpse more fully and more harrowingly what presences in the deepening winter of technique, in our cage which shows itself to be mournful in its essential being.

Bibliography

Agamben, Giorgio. Homo Sacer: Sovereign Power and Bare Life. Trans. by Daniel Heller-Roazen. Stanford: Stanford University Press, 1998.

_____. Means Without End: Notes on Politics. Trans. by Vincenzo Binetti and Cesare Casarino. Minneapolis: University of Minnesota Press, 2000.

_____. The Man Without Content. Trans. by Georgia Albert. Stanford: Stanford University Press,1999.

_____. The Time That Remains: A Commentary on the Letter to the Romans. Trans. by Patricia Dailey. Stanford: Stanford University Press, 2005.

Augustine of Hippo. Confessions. Trans. by Sir Tobie Matthew, Kt. London: Burns & Oates, 1954.

Baudrillard, Jean. Forget Foucault. New York: Semiotext(e), 1987.

_____. Simulacra and Simulation. Trans. by Sheila Faria Glaser. Michigan: University of Michigan Press, 2006.

_____. "Strike of Events." In Ctheory. Available at: http://www.ctheory.net/articles.aspx?id=52.

Benjamin, Walter. The Origin of the German Tragic Drama. Trans. by John Osbourne. New York: Verso, 1998.

Bryan, Bradley. "Bioethics, Biotechnology, and Liberalism: Problematizing Risk, Consent, and Law." In Law Health Journal. 11 (2003): 119-136.

_____. "Postmodernism and the Rationalization of Liberal Legal Culture." Discussion paper D98-9. Eco-Research Chair of Environmental Law and Policy, University of Victoria, August 1998. Available at: <http://www.polisproject.org/polis2/Discussion%20Papers/D98-9-PoMoLiberalLegalCulture.pdf>.

Cascardi, Anthony. The Subject of Modernity. Cambridge: Cambridge University Press, 1992.

Debord, Guy. The Society of the Spectacle. Trans. by Donald Nicholson-Smith. New York: Zone Books, 2006.

Deleuze, Gilles. The Logic of Sense. Ed. by Constantin V. Boundas and Mark Lester. Columbia University Press, 1990

Foster, M.B. "Christian Theology and Modern Science of Nature II." In Mind. 45:177 (January 1936): 1-28.

_____. "The Christian Doctrine of Creation and the Rise of Modern Natural Science." In Mind. 43:172. (Oct. 1934): 446-468.

Foucault, Michel. "Structuralism and Post-structuralism." In Foucault: Aesthetics, Method, and Epistemology. Ed. by James Faubion. Trans. by Robert Hurley et al. New York: The New Press, 1998.

Gadamer, Hans-Georg. The Idea of the Good in Platonic-Aristotelian Philosophy. Trans. by P. Christopher Smith. New Haven: Yale University Press, 1986.

Germain, Gilbert G. "The Revenge of the Sacred: Technology and Re-enchantment." In The Barbarism of Reason: Max Weber and the Twilight of Enlightenment. Ed. by Asher Horowitz and Terry Maley. University of Toronto Press, 1994.

Girard, René. Violence and the Sacred. Trans. by Patrick Gregory. Baltimore: John Hopkins University Press, 1979.

Goldman, Harvey. Max Weber and Thomas Mann: Calling and the Shaping of the Self. Berkeley: University of California Press, 1988.

Heidegger, Martin. Identity and Difference. Trans. by Joan Stambaugh. New York: Harper & Row, 1967.

_____. Poetry, Language, Thought. Trans. by Albert Hofstadter. New York: Perennial, 2001.

_____. The Basic Problems of Phenomenology. Trans. by Albert Hofstadter. Indiana University Press, 1982.

_____. The End of Philosophy. Trans. by Joan Stambaugh. New York: Harper & Row, 1973.

_____. The Question Concerning Technology and Other Essays. Trans. by William Lovitt. New York: Harper Colophon Books, 1977.

Hennis, Wilhelm. Max Weber, Essays in Reconstruction. Trans. by Keith Tribe. London: Allen & Unwin, 1988.

Kafka, Franz. Franz Kafka: The Complete Stories Ed. by Nahum N. Glatzer. New York: Schocken Books, 1971.

Kant, Immanuel. Critique of Judgment. Trans. by Werner S. Pluhar. Cambridge: Hackett Publishing Co., 1987.

_____. Groundwork for the Metaphysics of Morals. 2nd Edition. Trans. by Lewis White Beck. New Jersey: Prentice-Hall, 1997.

_____. Kant: Political Writings. Ed. by H.S. Reiss. Cambridge: Cambridge University Press, 2003.

Kelly, Duncan. The State of the Political: Conceptions of Politics and the State in the Thought of Max Weber, Carl Schmitt and Franz Neumann. Oxford University Press: 2003

Kontos, Alkis. "The World Disenchanted, and the Return of Gods and Demons." In The Barbarism of Reason. Ed. by Asher Horowitz and Terry Maley. University of Toronto Press, 1994.

Luther, Martin. Martin Luther on the Bondage of the Will: A New Translation of De Servo Arbitrio (1525), Martin Luther's Reply to Erasmus of Rotterdam. Trans. by J.I. Packer and O.R. Johnston. London: J. Clarke, 1957.

McCole, John. Walter Benjamin and the Antinomies of Tradition. Ithaca: Cornell University Press, 1993.

Maley, Terry. "Max Weber and the Iron Cage of Technology," in Bulletin of Science, Technology & Society 24:1 (Feb. 2004), esp. 74-5

_____. "The Politics of Time: Modernity and Subjectivity in Max Weber," in The Barbarism of Reason: Max Weber and the Twilight of Enlightenment. Ed. by Asher Horowitz and Terry Maley. University of Toronto Press, 1994.

Mommsen, Wolfgang J. Max Weber and German Politics 1890-1920. Trans. by Michael S. Steinberg. Chicago: University of Chicago Press, 1959.

Nietzsche, Friedrich. Thus Spoke Zarathustra: A Book For Everyone and No One. Trans. by R.J. Hollindale. New York: Penguin, 2003.

_____. Twilight of the Idols/The Anti-Christ. Trans. by R.J. Hollindale. New York: Penguin, 1968.

Offe, Claus. "Max Weber: American Escape Routes From the Iron Cage?" In Reflections on America. Trans. by Patrick Camiller. Cambridge: Polity, 2005.

Otto, Walter F. Dionysus: Myth and Cult. Trans. by Robert B. Palmer. Indiannapolis: Indiana University Press, 1965.

_____. Homeric Gods: The Spiritual Significance of Greek Religion. Trans. by Moses Hadas. London: Thames and Hudson, 1954.

Owen, David. Maturity and Modernity: Nietzsche, Weber, Foucault and the Ambivalence of Reason. New York: Routledge, 1994.

Palonen, Kari. "Max Weber's Reconceptualization of Freedom." In Political Theory 27:4 (Aug. 1999): 523-544.

Plato. Phaedrus & Letters VII and VIII. Trans. by Walter Hamilton. London: Penguin, 1973.

_____. "The Republic." In Great Dialogues of Plato. Trans. by W.H.D. Rouse. New York: Signet Classic, 1999.

Rose, Nikolas. "The Politics of Life Itself." In Theory, Culture, & Society. 18:6 (2001): 1-30.

Schaff, Lawrence A. Fleeing the Iron Cage: Culture, Politics, and Modernity in the Thought of Max Weber. Berkeley: University of California Press, 1989.

Schmitt, Carl. Political Theology. Trans. by George Schwab. University of Chicago Press, 2006.

Tenbruck, Friedrich H. "The Problem of Thematic Unity in the Works of Max Weber." In The British Journal of Sociology. 31:3, Special Issue (Sept. 1980): 316-351.

Titus Lucretius Carus. De Rerum Natura (On the Nature of Things). Trans. by William Ellery Leonard. Available at: < http://classics.mit.edu/Carus/nature_things.1.i.html> (June 4, 2007).

Walker, R.B.J. Inside/Outside: International Relations As Political Theory. Cambridge: Cambridge University Press, 1992.

Weber, Marianne. Max Weber: A Biography. Trans. by Harry Zohn. New York: Wiley, 1975.

Weber, Max. Ancient Judaism. Trans. by Hans H. Gerth and Don Martindale. Glencoe: The Free Press, 1952.

_____. Economy and Society: An Outline of Interpretive Sociology. Trans. by Ephraim Fischoff et al. Ed. by Guenther Roth and Claus Wittich. New York: Bedminster Press, 1968.

_____. From Max Weber: Essays in Sociology. Trans. and ed. by H.H. Gerth and C. Wright Mills. Routledge: 1957.

_____. The Methodology of the Social Sciences. Trans. and ed. by Edward A. Shik and Henry A.Finch. New York: The Free Press of Glencoe, 1949.

_____. The Protestant Ethic and the Spirit of Capitalism. Trans. by Talcott Parsons. New York: Charles Scribner's Sons, 1958.

_____. The Religion of China: Confucianism and Taoism. Trans. and ed. by Hans H. Gerth. New York: MacMillan, 1964.

_____. The Religion of India: The Sociology of Hinduism and Buddhism. Trans. and Ed. by Hans H. Gerth and Don Martindale. New York: The Free Press, 1958.

_____. The Theory of Social and Economic Organization trans. by A.M. Henderson and Talcott Parsons. Illinois: The Free Press, 1947.

_____. Weber: Political Writings. Ed. by Peter Lassman and Ronald Speirs. Cambridge: Cambridge University Press, 1994.

Williams, Michael C. The Realist Tradition and the Limits of International Relations. New York: Cambridge University Press, 2005.

Wolin, Sheldon S. "Max Weber: Legitimation, Method, and the Politics of Theory." In The Barbarism of Reason: Max Weber and the Twilight of Enlightenment. Ed. by Asher Horowitz and Terry Maley. University of Toronto Press, 1994.

Printed in the United States
149863LV00004B/40/P